THE
Sherlock Holmes
Victorian Cookbook

Favourite Recipes *of*
The Great Detective
& Dr Watson

THE

Sherlock Holmes

Victorian Cookbook

Favourite Recipes *of*
The Great Detective
& Dr Watson

William Bonnell

with an introduction
by Willy Brand

Macmillan Canada
TORONTO

Canadian Cataloguing in Publication Data

Bonnell, William, 1947 –
  The Sherlock Holmes Victorian cookbook: favourite recipes of the great detective and Dr. Watson

Includes index.
ISBN 0-7715-7412-6

1. Cookery, English. 2. Holmes, Sherlock (Fictitious character).
I. Title. II. Title: Victorian cookbook.

TX717.B66 1997   641.5941   C97-931227-2

1 2 3 4 5 FP 01 00 99 98 97

Cover and interior design by Bird-in-Hand Productions

The illustrations that appear on pages ii, vi, 2, 16, 60, 140, 156, 188, 190 and 196 are courtesy of the Metropolitan Toronto Reference Library.

Every effort has been made to ensure that all illustrative material is in the public domain. All inquiries concerning this matter should be directed to the publisher.

Macmillan Canada wishes to thank the Canada Council, the Ontario Ministry of Culture and Communications and the Ontario Arts Council for supporting its publishing program.

This book is available at special discounts for bulk purchases by your group or organization for sales promotions, premiums, fundraising and seminars.
For details, contact: Macmillan Canada, Special Sales Department,
29 Birch Avenue, Toronto, ON M4V 1E2. Tel: 416-963-8830.

Macmillan Canada
A Division of Canada Publishing Corporation
Toronto, Ontario, Canada

Printed in Canada

Contents

Foreword

... and presently, to my very great astonishment, a quite epicurean little cold supper began to be laid out upon our humble lodging-house mahogany. There were a couple of brace of cold woodcock, a pheasant, a pâté-de-foie-gras pie, with a group of ancient and cobwebby bottles ...

Just before nine o'clock Sherlock Holmes stepped briskly into the room. His features were gravely set, but there was a light in his eye which made me think that he had not been disappointed in his conclusions ...

"They have laid the supper, then," he said, rubbing his hands.

THE ADVENTURE OF THE NOBLE BACHELOR

r Watson's involvement with the investigations of his friend Sherlock Holmes seems to leave him in a perpetual state of astonishment. In this instance he appears to be overcome by what he and Holmes are about to eat. This is not quite the case. Both of these men were acquainted with the better cuisine of the day and had sampled the stuffed quails, roasted haunches of venison, and Italian truffles featured in the twelve-course dinners of the great Victorian country houses. They were also familiar with some of the finer restaurants, such as Simpson's—"our restaurant in the Strand" as Watson referred to it—with its well-deserved reputation for London's best roast beef and Yorkshire pudding.

However, they were more accustomed to the simpler fare provided by their steadfast landlady, Mrs Hudson. In *The Adventure of the Naval Treaty* Holmes claims that her Scottish cuisine "is a little limited," but Watson also notes that when one of her meals is set before him the Great Detective usually "falls hungrily upon it." That is understandable. Mrs Hudson's lamb chops with ginger sauce, Dundee cakes, shortbread, and scones with her own strawberry jam were undoubtedly delicious.

By the time Holmes set up his practice at 221b Baker Street, Britain's traditional morning repast of cheese, bread, and ale had given way to the "typical" English breakfast of porridge, bacon and eggs, toast, and marmalade. The mid-century introduction of a breed of Southeast Asian hen with an egg-laying capacity that far outstripped that of its domestic counterpart had much to do with this evolution. The boiled egg secured itself a place on the breakfast table, and Mrs Hudson's "lodging-house mahogany" would have been no exception. Middle-of-the-day luncheons, a habit earlier indulged by City merchants, had spread to the general populace, and the large-dinner hour was established at eight o'clock. This meal was preceded by a recent development—a five-o'clock tea consisting of cake, bread and butter, and honey or jam. Victorian society was highly regulated, and we can assume that when Holmes was not "on the chase" his day was rounded out by these four pillars of the contemporary diet.

One of the greatest culinary influences on British food in the nineteenth century was Alexis Soyer, a classical French chef who fled to England after the July Revolution of 1830, worked for various noblemen, then established his reputation as the chef de cuisine of the Reform Club. Here he designed the kitchens in such an impressive fashion that they became a tourist attraction once described by the Viscountess de Mallerville as "spacious as a ball-room, kept in the finest order, and white as a young bride." Soyer's other achievements included inventions such as the sink trap and a portable stove for the army in Crimea, several cookbooks, and a breakfast for two thousand produced for Queen Victoria's coronation in 1837. Holmes would have known of him through his famous bottled sauces—Soyer's Lady and Gentlemen's Sauce and Soyer's Relish, which became common in many households.

Sherlock Holmes was also no stranger to the foods hawked on London's streets. His investigations demanded he mingle with people from all stations of life in the largest and most cosmopolitan city of the world. For example, in *The Adventure of the Beryl Coronet* Watson observes him "dressed as a common loafer. With his collar turned up, his shiny seedy coat, his red cravat, and his worn boots, he was a perfect sample of the class." In these situations he likely dined on the boiled meat puddings, eel pies, pickled whelks, and other foods common to the working class.

But we have to bear in mind that in the more intense moments of a case he might forgo meals completely, although he often stopped for "a sandwich and a cup of coffee," as Watson notes in *The Red-Headed League*. The sandwich was popular in Victorian England, particularly on picnics and railway journeys. In the latter instance this can be put down to the infamous quality of railway catered food, something Alexis Soyer once described as "bad as any human being could possibly make it." We can be assured that Mrs Hudson provided Holmes and Watson with many fine potted beef and smoked salmon pâté sandwiches before they climbed on board a railway carriage.

Beau Brummel, the fashion plate of the Regency period

(1811–20), was reluctant to admit that he had once eaten a pea. Fortunately, neither Brummel nor any of his constipated contemporaries arbitrated fashion or dining habits by the time Holmes first donned his deerstalker; vegetables were no longer considered vulgar and the vegetable garden had a significant role in Victorian society. However, many of the dishes Holmes and Watson ate were prepared according to directions largely unaltered since medieval times. This would have often been the case with cakes, meats, and sauces. It was particularly true for fare served during the festive seasons of the year, and we can be sure that Mrs Hudson served her two lodgers with a Christmas goose roasted according to very traditional directions. Did she also offer them haggis, the oatmeal and internal organ mixture prepared in a sheep's stomach, during Hogmanay? Perhaps not. Some Sherlockian commentators feel that Dr Watson was of Scottish descent on his mother's side, and the presence of a plate of haggis at 221b Baker Street would not have proven a severe test for his much exercised faculties of astonishment, although it might have come as quite a surprise to his famous table companion. But surely they both tasted her black bun, the famous cake served on Twelfth Night, and Atholl brose, the old Scottish beverage of oatmeal, honey, and whisky. Whatever their inspiration, be it Mrs Hudson's heritage or, as is the case with Dr Watson's Favourite Chutney, the good doctor's early sojourn in India with the British army, the recipes in *The Sherlock Holmes Victorian Cookbook* have all been adapted, where necessary, to contemporary tastes. Victorian flavourings and spice preparations, particularly for savoury dishes, were sometimes very powerful. A similar effort has been made to reduce quantities. The households of Holmes's time were usually large, and "receipts," when they were written down at all, often called for ingredients for up to twenty people.

George Bernard Shaw, a contemporary of Holmes's creator, Sir Arthur Conan Doyle, once said, "There is no love sincerer than the love of food." This book has been written out of a love for Victorian cooking and the adventures of Sherlock Holmes. I hope it will add to the reader's enjoyment of both.

~WILLIAM BONNELL

ACKNOWLEDGEMENTS

Writing may be largely a solitary pursuit, but no book is ever written without the support of others, and I would like to thank the following people for their contributions to my efforts with this manuscript:

Willy Brand for his inspiration and participation. His culinary skills and grasp of the profound role of cuisine in culture have had an enormous influence on several generations of Canadian cooks and chefs.

The staff of Macmillan Canada for their enthusiasm and very professional assistance, particularly Susan Girvan and Ann Nelles.

Victoria Gill, Curator of the Arthur Conan Doyle Collection at the Metropolitan Toronto Reference Library, for her advice and Sherlockian scholarship.

Tony Hawke and Hugh Carter for their proposal suggestions.

The patient librarians of the Guildwood Branch of the Scarborough Public Library system for their flexible approach to renewals.

Mr and Mrs Hurd of Parry Sound for their help with some of the more fleet-footed of game ingredients.

Joan Henry and Holly Briesmaster for the loan of two very useful books of traditional recipes.

Many friends and family for their willingness to endure the prolonged trials of recipe testing. And most of all, Clare, who has always been there.

Introduction

I have found it very enjoyable to sort, adjust, and test the recipes that have made their way into The Sherlock Holmes Victorian Cookbook.

In my experience cooking has always been an amalgam of craft and art. The craft lies in the measurement of weights, volumes, and temperatures, areas with which the cook must be concerned while acknowledging the scientific limits of cuisine. Temperatures, for example, will always vary from one oven to another, and the heat-conducting qualities of glass, stainless steel, aluminum, and other metals are very different. Imperial measures differ between the Commonwealth, Britain, and the United States, and the Canadian metric use of millilitres is not practiced in Europe. Books written for professional cooks measure by weight, a method that allows for precision for the occupational expert, although it is of little help to the household cook without scales.

However, cooking should be enjoyable for people, and it would be sheer drudgery for everyone if cookbooks were technical manuals for a cuisine variation of painting by numbers. They must be a pleasure to read, and their recipes should be approached as guidelines that encourage individual artistic creativity.

What is important about The Sherlock Holmes Victorian Cookbook *is its fascinating blend of history, literature, and cuisine. Some of the recipes are familiar to me from my own cooking career. They are old friends, while others that are less familiar have become new and interesting acquaintances. The promise of this book is that it will enable a cook to experience the richness and cultural traditions of a cuisine from an earlier era, and contribute to an enjoyment and love of cooking. What more could one ask for?*

WILLY BRAND, M.C.A. (MASTER OF CULINARY ARTS)
C.C.C. (CANADIAN CERTIFIED CHEF)

Soups

"Excuse the admiration of a connoisseur," said he, as he waved his hand towards the line of portraits which covered the opposite wall. "Watson won't allow that I know anything of art, but that is mere jealousy, because our views on the subject differ…

"Who is the gentleman with the telescope?"

"That is Rear-Admiral Baskerville, who served under Rodney in the West Indies."

THE HOUND OF THE BASKERVILLES

n examination of Sir Henry Baskerville's family portraits provided Holmes with an important clue in his hunt for the villain behind the fiendish "hound" that terrorized the Baskervilles. Rear-Admiral Baskerville, however, a man with impressive maritime credentials, was one of the more benign of Sir Henry's ancestors and must have played a vital role in keeping the trade goods flowing between Britain and one of her more important colonies. Ships returning from the West Indies carried, along with other commodities, molasses, spices, rum, and sugar. A more unusual, but very popular, cargo, kept alive during the voyage in large tanks of fresh water, were West Indian green turtles. These melancholy creatures, weighing anywhere from 50 to 600 pounds, were destined for the soup pots of the wealthy. Mrs Beeton notes in her 1861 *Book of Household Management* that "hundreds of tureens of turtle soup are served annually at the Lord Mayor's dinner in Guildhall." It was also about this time that mock turtle soup, based on veal or mutton and served in turtle shells, became the vogue among the less prosperous.

By Holmes's day the soup dish was institutionalized as the first course at the better dinner parties, and was understood as a litmus test of the talents in the resident kitchen, providing guests with a foreknowledge of what remained in store for them in the succeeding courses. There was usually a choice of one thick and one clear (consommé), the latter involving several days of clarification with egg whites, egg shells, and sieves of fine cloth.

The creation of a soup in earlier periods of British cookery was usually not such a trial. They were basically gruels and pottages of boiled grains and cereals. Some of these were part of the "leechdoms"—collections of Anglo-Saxon remedies used to ward off diseases and bodily complaints. Garlic simmered in "hen broth," for example, was used to cure intestinal ailments. Occasionally meat sauces were strained, mixed with wine, reheated with chopped stewed meat and served over pieces of bread known as sops. In France, *soupe* referred to the original liquid base of the dish, and the word *soup* was applied to the thin pottages that became fashionable among the English gentry in the late seventeenth century. Cooked broth was strained and served with vermicelli, light vegetables, and pieces of poultry or meat.

The more delicate touch of French cuisine was also felt in Scotland, where the influence of the "auld alliance" supplemented the traditional heavy brose (oatmeal), barley, and grain-based pottages with others of a lighter consistency. The Soup à la Reine recipe in this chapter is one of the better known of these lighter Scottish soups.

A later development was the "Portable" or "Pocket" soup, made by reducing a strong stock—usually veal-based—to a thick glue-like consistency. Captain Cook was one of the first to make use of portable soup and had cases of it on board during his voyage to the South Pacific in 1772. It was served by adding boiling water and pease flour. Rear-Admiral Baskerville would have known it, and Jonathan Small, the convict treasure looter whom Holmes and Watson chased along the Thames in a police launch in *The Sign of Four* affair, might have become familiar with it in his voyages in the Near and Far East.

In 1847 two men named Davidson and Symington took out a patent on their new method of producing dried foods and established a line of Symington's Desiccated Soups. Perhaps Holmes boiled up some of their product over his "rude grate," as Watson put it, when he was camping out in a neolithic hut on the lonely moors during the Baskerville investigation. However, by that time dried soups were commonly retailed by many grocers and might have even found their way into the larder of the discriminating landlady at 221b Baker Street. 🍎

Asparagus with Pale Ale

"… They drove away in different directions and I went off to make my own arrangements."

"Which are?"

"Some cold beef and a glass of beer," he answered, ringing the bell. "I have been too busy to think of food, and I am likely to be busier still this evening. By the way, Doctor, I shall want your cooperation."

"I shall be delighted."

A SCANDAL IN BOHEMIA

*A*s Victorian men, both Holmes and Watson enjoyed their beef and beer, and they would have been partial to this soup, which is based on a recipe that appears in Mrs Beeton's *Book of Household Management* (1861).

Serves 4–6

> 2 lb (1 kg) lean beef, diced
> 2 tbsp (25 mL) all-purpose flour
> 2 tbsp (25 mL) butter
> 5 cups (1.25 L) beef stock
> 1 cup (250 mL) pale ale or beer
> 1 tsp (5 mL) salt
> 1 tsp (5 mL) dried marjoram

1/2 tsp (2 mL) dried mint
2 cups (500 mL) chopped fresh spinach (or
    1/4 lb/125 g frozen chopped spinach)
2 bunches asparagus stalks (approx. 1 lb/500 g)
1 tsp (5 mL) sugar
Salt and pepper to taste

Dust the beef with the flour. Melt the butter in a large saucepan over medium heat, and cook the meat until it browns on all sides. Add the stock, ale, and 1 tsp (5 mL) salt. Bring to a boil, then reduce the heat and simmer, covered, for 30 minutes.

Add the marjoram, mint, and spinach. Bring to a boil again, then reduce the heat. Cut the top 3 inches (8 cm) from the asparagus stalks and chop them into bite-sized pieces (the remainder of the stalks can be saved for vegetable stock). Add the asparagus tops to the soup and simmer until they are tender (4–5 minutes). Stir in the sugar. Season with salt and pepper. Serve hot. ❦

Baker Street
Scotch Barley Broth

"Now, Watson, if you will pack your bag I will cable to Mrs Hudson to make one of her best efforts for two hungry travellers at seven-thirty tomorrow."

THE DISAPPEARANCE OF LADY FRANCES CARFAX

Holmes was in a hurry to leave Montpelier in France, where the trail of the abducted Lady Frances Carfax had gone cold. Once back in Baker Street he knew he could take up the search in London, where he was certain her kidnappers had taken his client. Mrs Hudson, upon receiving his cable, might well have thought this hearty and traditional Scottish soup the perfect fare for her two lodgers as they returned to continue the rigours of their investigations.

Serves 4–6

> 1 1/2-lb (750 g) whole cheap cut of beef (neck or
>   other stewing portion)
> 1 onion, chopped
> 3 tbsp (50 mL) dried split peas, soaked overnight
> 2 tbsp (25 mL) pearl barley
> 7 cups (1.75 L) water

1 tsp (5 mL) salt
1 medium carrot, sliced
1/3 medium turnip, diced
2 leeks (white parts only), trimmed and sliced
1/4 cup (50 mL) chopped fresh parsley
1 tsp (5 mL) sugar
Salt and pepper

Remove any fat from the meat. Put meat into a large saucepan along with the onion, drained peas, pearl barley, water, and salt. Bring to a boil and reduce the heat, cover, and simmer for 1 hour. Remove the meat, dice it coarsely, and return it to the pan.

Add the carrot and turnip. Simmer, uncovered, for 5 minutes. Add the leeks; simmer for another 5 minutes or until all the vegetables are tender. Stir in the parsley, sugar, and salt and pepper to taste.

Serve with fresh warm rolls and butter.

Note: Scotch Barley Broth is sometimes made with lamb, and on occasion the meat is served as a separate course. ❦

Imperial Mulligatawny

"I'm a Worcestershire man myself, born near Pershore ... I got into a mess over a girl and could only get out of it by taking the Queen's shilling and joining the Third Buffs, which was just starting for India."

THE SIGN OF FOUR

So begins the embittered confession of Jonathan Small, a man whose days in India were remarkable but tragic. Shortly after his arrival he lost a leg to a crocodile while swimming in the Ganges River, and was later swept up in the 1857–58 sepoy mutiny against the British. Then, he was convicted of murder in the theft of the Great Agra treasure and spent twenty miserable years in captivity.

India left its mark on Dr Watson as well. However, his interlude there, although not without its difficulties, in no way resembled the deplorable sojourn of Small. In fact, as time went by Watson seemed to take pleasure in recounting his Indian adventures to friends and acquaintances.

Mulligatawny soup is originally from Southern India. Its name is derived from two Tamil words—*molegoo* and *tunnee*, meaning water and pepper, and it would have certainly rekindled Dr Watson's memories of his army days in the most glittering possession of Queen Victoria's Empire.

Serves 4–6

3 tbsp (50 mL) butter
2 lb (1 kg) lean beef, cut in bite-sized pieces
7 cups (1.75 L) water
1 tsp (5 mL) mustard seeds
1 tsp (5 mL) ground coriander
1 tsp (5 mL) cumin
1 tsp (5 mL) fenugreek
1 medium onion, chopped
1 medium carrot, diced
1/4 medium turnip, diced (about 1 cup/250 mL)
1 stalk celery, sliced
1 green pepper, chopped
1 apple, peeled and chopped
Salt and pepper

Melt half of the butter in a large saucepan over medium heat and brown the meat on all sides. Add 4 cups (1 L) of the water, bring to a boil, and simmer, covered, for 45 minutes. Remove from heat and add the remaining 3 cups (750 mL) of water to help the broth cool. Strain the broth, put the meat to one side, and skim any fat off the broth.

Melt the remaining butter in the same saucepan over medium heat. Cook the mustard seeds, stirring, for 30 seconds. Add the coriander, cumin, and fenugreek; cook for 30 seconds. Add the onion, carrot, turnip, celery, and green pepper; cook for 2 minutes, stirring to cover the vegetables with spices. Stir in the apple and cook for another minute.

Add the reserved broth and meat. Bring to a quick boil, then simmer gently, uncovered, for 10 minutes or until the vegetables are tender. Season with salt and pepper. Serve hot. 🍎

Soup à la Reine

"But, none the less, my turn in that way is in my veins, and may have come with my grandmother, who was the sister of Vernet, the French artist. Art in the blood is liable to take the strangest forms."

THE ADVENTURE OF THE GREEK INTERPRETER

*H*olmes here ascribes his aptitude for deduction to his French ancestors. We know that he spoke French well enough to pass himself off as a French labourer, undertake a commission for the French government, and work for several months in a laboratory in southern France while he was evading Professor Moriarty's murderous henchmen after the famous struggle at Reichenbach Fall. His familiarity with Gallic culture and traditions meant that he would have been very interested in the French culinary influences on Mrs Hudson's Scottish recipes.

Soup à la Reine is also known as Lorraine Soup after Mary of Guise-Lorraine, who married James V in 1538 and brought her French chefs and servants with her to Scotland. This recipe is one of the many products of that cross-pollination of cuisines.

Serves 4–6

2 cups (500 mL) chopped cooked chicken
6 cups (1.5 L) chicken stock
1/3 cup (75 mL) finely ground almonds
1/4 cup (50 mL) fine white dry breadcrumbs
1 tsp (5 mL) sugar
1 tsp (5 mL) salt
1/2 tsp (2 mL) pepper
2/3 cup (150 mL) table (18%) cream

Blend the chicken smooth with 1 cup (250 mL) of the stock in a blender or food processor. Put it into a saucepan and add the rest of the chicken stock. Stir in the ground almonds, breadcrumbs, sugar, salt, and pepper. Bring to a boil, then stir in the cream. Reduce the heat and simmer gently, uncovered, for 5 more minutes. Adjust the seasoning and serve hot.

Note: An old stewing hen simmered for about an hour is an excellent source of the meat and stock needed for this recipe. It is important that the chicken stock be very well flavoured, otherwise the soup may be somewhat bland. 🍎

Old-Fashioned Pea Soup

"No good, my dear Watson. This, the best and only final clue, has run to nothing. But, indeed, I have little doubt that we can build up a sufficient case without it. By Jove! my dear fellow, it is nearly nine, and the landlady babbled of green peas at seven-thirty."

THE ADVENTURE OF THE THREE STUDENTS

*T*he landlady in question here is not Mrs Hudson but the owner of lodgings in "one of our great University towns," where Holmes and Watson were staying when they were asked to help avert a scandal in the making over the theft of an important examination paper for the Fortescue Scholarship. How their landlady served their green peas is not detailed, but a substantial pea soup similar to the one in this eighteenth-century recipe would have been very nourishing for both of them.

Serves 8–10

> 6 cups (1.5 L) dried whole green peas, soaked
>   overnight
> 15 cups (3.75 L) water
> 4 celery stalks, roughly chopped
> 1 cup (250 mL) roughly chopped lettuce leaves
>   (head, green leaf, or romaine)

2 tsp (10 mL) dried mint
3 tbsp (50 mL) butter
3 medium onions, chopped
2 medium cucumbers, peeled, seeded, and chopped
3 cups (750 mL) fresh or frozen green peas
Salt and pepper
1/2 cup (125 mL) table (18%) cream
Croutons

Place drained peas in a large soup pot with the water, celery, lettuce, and mint. Cover and boil until the peas are completely tender (approx. 45 minutes). Purée and return to the pot.

Melt the butter in a saucepan over medium heat and cook the onions and cucumbers, stirring occasionally, until the onions are soft. Purée the vegetables, then add them to the pea purée. Bring to a boil, then add the fresh peas and cook gently for 10 minutes. Add salt and pepper to taste. Ladle into soup bowls and add a tablespoon of cream to each serving. Serve the croutons separately.

Note: If a smaller quantity of soup is desired, simply reduce all the ingredients by half. However, it is just as easy to make a large quantity and it freezes well for future use. ❧

Salads and Vegetables

We made our way downstairs as quietly as possible, and out into the bright morning sunshine. In the road stood our horse and trap, with the half-clad stable-boy waiting at the head. We both sprang in, and away we dashed down the London Road. A few country carts were stirring, bearing in vegetables to the metropolis, but the lines of villas on either side were as silent and lifeless as some city in a dream.

THE MAN WITH THE TWISTED LIP

he country carts noticed by Dr Watson were probably going to Covent Garden, London's largest vegetable market of the day. Originally an orchard plot belonging to the monks of Westminster, it was purchased by the Earl of Bedford and developed by the fourth earl, who engaged Inigo Jones to lay out the church of St Paul's and a piazza on the property. In 1670 the earl's son obtained a licence to hold a market in the piazza. Covent Garden's main rival was Spitalfields, which was supplied with vegetables from gardens in Lewisham and Blackheath and with potatoes by Irish farmers who rented fields to the east of the city in Wanstead and Ilford.

The idea of market gardens as major sources of produce for nearby cities came from immigrant Flemish and French gardeners who brought with them their experience of commercial gardens on the outskirts of their native cities. This led to the development of similar rings of gardens around the larger British towns and cities. The Flemish and French, however, were not the first to bring their gardening habits to Britain. The Romans introduced garlic, garden onions, radishes, leeks, lettuces, and a powerful salad dressing of cumin, ginger, rue, pepper, honey, and vinegar. The salad habit seems to have weathered centuries of social change, for there are fourteenth-century recipes for salad mixtures of parsley, sage, garlic, onion, borage, fennel, rosemary, and several other herbs. These ingredients were augmented in the sixteenth and seventeenth centuries with petals of violets, primroses, cowslips, nasturtiums, and a number of other flowers.

Tomatoes made their appearance in the seventeenth century, but, as members of the deadly nightshade family, they were regarded as dangerous—although in some quarters they were thought to have interesting aphrodisiac properties—and it was more than a hundred years before they played even a minimal role in British cuisine. Sweet potatoes, imported from Spain (the Spanish had discovered them in South America), were also thought to be aphrodisiac and were usually baked in rich, sweet pies. The "Virginian" potato, the plant that sustained the enormous population growth of the Victorian years, was introduced during the Elizabethan reign, and pumpkins were brought over from France in the late sixteenth century, replacing the coarse gourds of the medieval period. Cucumbers also reappeared at this time, having died out when the villa-type gardens of the Romans collapsed with their departure.

A long-held prejudice against vegetables in some quarters of British society was gradually dispelled in the nineteenth century. Some of this suspicion was rooted in class attitudes; the aristocracy had a tendency to disdain vegetables as peasant fodder, and the wealthy gentry of the Industrial Revolution looked upon heavy meat consumption as a measure of their newly arrived social worth. Certain vegetables, such as leeks and onions, were also known to "taint the breath," and there was a personal concern with embarrassing emissions brought on by the possible indigestibility of others not rigorously boiled.

This suspicion of vegetables may also have been reflective of an historical distaste for the traditional, very tough, and fibrous root vegetables that were native to Britain and only gradually displaced by more tender varieties from abroad, something Isabella Beeton, the most influential of Victorian food writers, refers to as "a share of the blessings of other climates ... enabling us to participate in the luxury which a more genial sun has produced."

By Holmes's day, vegetables and various salads were served in the better taverns and restaurants, and kitchen gardens were important to many rural families. Great estates sometimes employed dozens of gardeners whose job it was to supply the manor kitchens with vegetables year round. Urban households, such as Mrs Hudson's, would have purchased their "greens" at the local green-grocer. This individual likely bought his in bulk at one of the larger markets such as Covent Garden and Spitalfields, which in their turn relied on the country carts Dr Watson saw that bright and silent morning "bearing in vegetables to the metropolis." ❧

Artichokes in Batter

"Yes; when I went to see if the door was fastened for the night I met her slipping in. I saw the man, too, in the gloom."
"Do you know him?"
"Oh, yes; he is the green-grocer who brings our vegetables round. His name is Frances Prosper."

THE ADVENTURE OF THE BERYL CORONET

*I*n the Beryl Coronet affair Holmes discovers that the local green-grocer is really Sir George Burnwell, a cunning philanderer and jewel thief who has made off with a precious beryl coronet entrusted to the respectable banker Alexander Holder. In fact, the local Victorian green-grocer was generally a benign individual who supplied his customers with available fresh produce. One vegetable in constant demand during Holmes's day was the artichoke. The recipe below is a variation of one that was common at that time.

Serves 4 as an appetizer

1 cup (250 mL) all-purpose flour
1 tsp (5 mL) salt
1/4 tsp (1 mL) pepper
1 egg
3/4 cup (175 mL) milk
3 tbsp (50 mL) oil
8 canned artichoke hearts, rinsed and drained
3 tbsp (50 mL) chopped fresh parsley

In a large bowl, sift the flour, salt, and pepper. In a small bowl, beat together the egg, milk, and 1 tbsp (15 mL) of the oil. Add the liquid to the flour mixture and beat until the batter is smooth.

Heat the remaining oil in a deep frying pan over high heat. Dip each artichoke heart in the batter and fry until the batter just begins to brown. Drain, and serve warm sprinkled with the parsley.

Note: Canned artichokes are already tender and require no additional cooking. 🍎

German Dressed Carrots

"Sarasate plays at the St James's Hall this afternoon," he remarked. "What do you think, Watson? Could your patients spare you for a few hours?"

"I have nothing to do today. My practice is never very absorbing."

"Then put on your hat and come. I am going through the City first, and we can have some lunch on the way. I observe that there is a good deal of German music on the programme, which is rather more to my taste than Italian or French. It is introspective, and I want to introspect. Come along!"

THE RED-HEADED LEAGUE

The trip Holmes and Watson take through the City is an important part of an investigation into an elaborate tunnelling operation undertaken to steal bullion from a bank in Saxe-Coburg Square. Prince Albert, Queen Victoria's husband, was from the Saxe-Coburg family and his contributions to British life included German customs such as the Christmas tree. In this Victorian carrot recipe, the use of the onion is an example of German influence on British eating habits. Perhaps Prince Albert also expressed an interest in carrots cooked in this manner. In any case, this is a tasty way to prepare an often too plainly served vegetable.

Serves 4

6 large carrots
3 tbsp (50 mL) butter
1 tbsp (15 mL) minced fresh parsley
1 tbsp (15 mL) finely chopped onion
1/2 tsp (2 mL) salt
1/4 tsp (1 mL) nutmeg
1 1/2 cups (375 mL) beef stock
2 tbsp (25 mL) all-purpose flour

Slice the carrots no thicker than 1/4 inch (5 mm). Melt half of the butter in a saucepan over medium heat. Add the carrots, parsley, onion, salt, and nutmeg; cook, stirring, for 2 minutes, making sure carrots are well saturated with butter. Pour in the beef stock and simmer, uncovered, until the carrots are almost tender (3–5 minutes). Drain the carrots in a sieve, and reserve the carrots and the stock.

Melt the remaining butter in the saucepan over medium heat. Add the flour, stirring for 1 minute to make a smooth paste. Gradually add the stock while stirring and simmer, stirring, until the mixture thickens. Gently stir in the carrots and simmer until tender. Serve hot. ❦

Musgrave Ritual Mushrooms

"Altogether there are eight maids, the cook, the butler, two footmen, and a boy. The garden and the stables, of course, have a separate staff."

THE ADVENTURE OF THE MUSGRAVE RITUAL

*I*n the Musgrave Ritual affair Holmes undertook an investigation on behalf of Reginald Musgrave, an old university acquaintance from an aristocratic lineage who lived in the ancestral manor of Hurlstone, a considerable property that demanded a large staff for its upkeep. One of the duties of the gardening staff of Victorian households was the care and cultivation of the mushroom crop. Mushrooms were a breakfast favourite, and to keep the kitchens well supplied the gardener cultivated them from spawn in forcing houses on beds of fermented manure and wheelbarrows of soil collected from mole hills. Nowadays the complications of growing mushrooms can be left to those large commercial enterprises that make them available year round in most supermarkets.

Serves 4 as a breakfast side dish

24

3/4 lb (375 g) mushrooms
3 tbsp (50 mL) unsalted butter
1/2 tsp (2 mL) salt
1/4 tsp (1 mL) white pepper
Juice of half a lemon (about 1 tbsp/15 mL)
1 tbsp (15 mL) all-purpose flour
2 tbsp (25 mL) table (18%) cream
1/4 tsp (1 mL) nutmeg

Trim off and discard the bottom of the mushroom stems. Cut each mushroom in half.

Melt the butter in a saucepan over medium heat and add the mushrooms, salt, pepper, and lemon juice. Cover and cook the mushrooms until they are almost tender (about 2 minutes). Add the flour and cook, stirring, for 1 minute, then add the cream, stirring until the sauce thickens. Stir in the nutmeg and serve hot. 🍎

Lemon Beetroot Tops

The Manor House, with its many gables and its small diamond-paned windows, was still much as the builder had left it in the early seventeenth century. Of the double moats which had guarded its more warlike predecessor, the outer had been allowed to dry up, and served the humble function of a kitchen garden.

THE VALLEY OF FEAR

John Douglas, an American, purchased the Manor House of Birlstone after it had been untenanted for many years. Douglas was later murdered by criminals connected to the infamous Professor Moriarity, and the Manor House and its garden were left with a friend. Little is said of what was grown in the kitchen garden, although there can be no doubt that beetroots, a popular year-round vegetable, could be found there.

Beetroot tops are very nutritious and are usually sold with bunches of beetroots in supermarkets. The younger beetroot tops from smaller beets are sweeter, and since the stems are smaller the whole top may be cooked more easily.

Serves 4

> 8 cups (2 L) young beetroot tops (from 1 large
>   bunch of beetroots)
> 1 tsp (5 mL) salt
> 1 tbsp (15 mL) butter
> 1 tsp (5 mL) sugar
> 4 tsp (20 mL) lemon juice

Wash the beetroot tops well to remove any grit. Bring to a boil 2 quarts (2 L) of water. Stir in salt and beetroot tops; cook until just tender. Drain and return beetroot tops to the pot. Toss with the butter, sugar, and lemon juice. Serve immediately. ❧

Rumbledethumps

"And so, my dear Watson, we have ended by turning the dancing men to good when they have so often been the agents of evil ... Three-forty is our train, and I fancy we should be back in Baker Street for dinner."

THE ADVENTURE OF THE DANCING MEN

*H*olmes seems anxious to be back in Baker Street after his successful dispatch of the mystery of the "dancing men" code and the death of Hilton Cubbit in Norfolk. However, there is no indication that Mrs Hudson was given any advance notice of his arrival. She might well have had to fall back on some of her simpler Scottish dishes such as rumbledethumps, a Scottish version of the Irish colcannon potato dish. The name rumbledethump is a combination of *rumble*, to mix, and *thump*, to bash together, something she might have been tempted to do with lodgers returning unannounced and demanding dinner.

Serves 4–6

> 6 medium baking potatoes, peeled
> 1/2 cup (125 mL) hot milk
> 1/4 cup (50 mL) butter
> 2 cups (500 mL) cooked shredded green cabbage
> 2 tbsp (25 mL) chopped chives
> Salt and pepper
> 1/2 cup (125 mL) shredded Cheddar cheese

In a saucepan, boil the potatoes in salted water until tender; drain well and mash the potatoes thoroughly. Stir in the hot milk and the butter. Stir in the cabbage, chives, and salt and pepper to taste. Spread the mixture in a pie plate and sprinkle on the cheese. Bake at 350°F (180°C) for 20 minutes or until the top begins to brown. ❦

Salmagundi

*It was on a bitterly cold and frosty morning during the winter of '97
that I was awakened by a tugging at my shoulder. It was Holmes …*
*"Come, Watson, come!" he cried. "The game is afoot. Not a word!
Into your clothes and come!"*

THE ADVENTURE OF THE ABBEY GRANGE

*T*he winter weather never deterred Holmes when an investigation beckoned, but it would have provided some difficulties for
Mrs Hudson. Fresh produce was not easy to come by in the cold
months, and a Victorian cook had to make do with what there
was. Salmagundi (sometimes corrupted to Solomongundy) is
derived from seventeenth century salads that included a large
variety of meats and fish. The recipe below is for a winter salad
that uses pickled vegetables and allows for attractive contrasts
of colour on a serving plate.

Serves 4

> 1 1/2 cups (375 mL) diced cooked chicken
> 4 medium pickled beetroots, sliced
> 4 hard-boiled eggs, sliced
> 1 1/2 cups (375 mL) lean ham cut in thin strips
> 3 medium potatoes, peeled, boiled, and sliced
> 1 1/2 cups (375 mL) chopped pickled red cabbage
> 1/2 cup (125 mL) chopped fresh parsley
> Light oil and vinegar salad dressing

Put the chicken in the centre of a large plate or on individual
salad plates. Circle it with a ring of the sliced beetroot, then a
ring of hard-boiled eggs, then ham, potatoes, and pickled cabbage. Sprinkle with the parsley. Serve at room temperature. Serve
the dressing separately. ❦

Fish and Seafood

Our boilers were strained to the utmost and the frail shell vibrated and creaked with the fierce energy which was driving us along. We had shot through the pool, past the West India Docks, down the long Deptford Reach, and up again after rounding the Isle of Dogs. The dull blur in front of us resolved itself clearly into the dainty Aurora ... At Greenwich we were about three hundred paces behind them. At Blackwall we couldn't have been more than two hundred and fifty. I have coursed many creatures in many countries during my chequered career, but never did sport give me such a wild thrill as this mad, flying man-hunt down the Thames.

THE SIGN OF FOUR

Watson is referring to a river chase in pursuit of the convict adventurer Jonathan Small and the stolen Great Agra treasure. The pursuit ended near the "melancholy Plumstead Marshes," with the capture of Small and the loss overboard of the fabulous treasure. By that time Watson and Holmes had covered a considerable stretch of the Thames and had passed some of London's most renowned landmarks, including many of the important bridges and docks, the Tower, St Paul's Cathedral, and a number of Wren churches. Watson mentions Greenwich, the location of mean time for the entire world, but also well known for its huge shoals of whitebait—small, silvery fry that were floured, then deep-fried and seasoned with lemon juice, and served as a delicacy with iced champagne. To this day whitebait is still served in Greenwich in the restored Trafalgar Tavern, built in 1830. They also passed the famous Billingsgate fish market, an official "free and open market" since 1699, and a site where seafood had been sold during much of the Thames's history. During Holmes's day hucksters would trundle their barrows of seafood up Fish Street Hill and sell fish and shellfish in the streets.

Seafood has always played a major role in the British diet. During the Roman occupation British oysters acquired a fame that prompted their shipment back to Rome itself, and the soil under Roman sites is often layered with the shells of seafood consumed by the Imperial legions. But it was the fast days of the Christian church—Wednesdays, Fridays, Saturdays, and Lent up until the late Middle Ages—that stimulated the greatest demand for fish, particularly for Britain's schools of coastal herring. In addition, the eel and salmon fisheries were to become so important that both commodities were used as rent payments, and salmon was such a day-to-day food in some areas that labourers and servants demanded contracts stipulating they would not be served it more than three times a week. Inland ponds, first developed by monastic orders to harvest local freshwater species, became a common feature of manorial life, and households kept a fisherman on staff who caught fish from the owner's pond whenever they were needed.

Perishability and poor transportation meant that a great deal of seafood was preserved by pickling, smoking, or salting and salted cod made up 60 percent of the fish eaten in England. The abolition of compulsory fish days following Henry VIII's break with Rome led to a gradual decline in the demand for both salted and fresh fish, and many of the coarser freshwater species, such as chub and roach, were dropped from the diet altogether, leaving inland millponds and lakes to become ornamental waters. However, the coming of the railways reinvigorated the fishing industry. By the beginning of the nineteenth century fresh Scottish salmon, previously smoked or salted, began to arrive in London in boxes of ice, but salmon pickled in vinegar did remain popular throughout the Victorian period. Oysters, fresh or pickled, were in great demand, but the effects of early pollution eventually exhausted the natural beds and they had to be revived by artificial breeding.

During the years in which Holmes undertook his investigations thousands of tons of cockles were gathered along the northern coasts—often by husband and wife teams with a horse and small cart—and sent down by rail to London. There they were served along with bowls of shrimp, mussels, whelks, winkles, and jellied eels in the famous shellfish stalls in the Cockney areas of the city with which Holmes was intimately familiar. It is easy to picture him in one of the working-class disguises he liked to adopt, tucking into a dish of stewed eels in parsley sauce in one of the many eel and pie shops found in London in those days. Or perhaps he availed himself of the fish and chip meal that had gained such popularity after "chipped" potatoes were introduced from France in the 1870s. We cannot be sure, but we do know that by the time he began his famous career, seafood was once again prominent in the diet not only of those living in the fascinating and somewhat sinister metropolis where he worked, but throughout all of Britain. 🦐

Baked Stuffed Pike

"Yes, we should have a full day to-day," he remarked, and he rubbed his hands with the joy of action. "The nets are all in place, and the drag is about to begin. We'll know before the day is out whether we have caught our big, lean-jawed pike, or whether he has got through the meshes."

THE HOUND OF THE BASKERVILLES

*H*olmes is referring here not to an actual fish but to Stapleton, the criminal mind behind the fiendish hound that terrified Sir Henry Baskerville. It is interesting that he used a pike to describe his enemy; he had some knowledge of fishing as a gentleman's form of recreation. In the Shoscombe Old Place affair he and Watson probably took an opportunity to catch a few of the pike known to lurk in Hall Lake in Shoscombe Park following that particular investigation.

Pike is not always a favourite fish because of the limitless number of small bones present in smaller specimens. However, this is much less of a problem with a pike of reasonable size (4–5 lb/2–2.2 kg), and the flesh, although it can be slightly on the dry side, is very tasty.

Serves 4–6

3 tbsp (50 mL) butter
1/4 cup (50 mL) chopped onion
8 fresh or frozen oysters (not smoked), chopped
1/4 cup (50 mL) fresh chopped parsley
1 tsp (5 mL) salt
2 turns of pepper from a pepper mill
    (or 1/2 tsp/2 mL ground pepper)
1/2 tsp (2 mL) mace
4 cups (1 L) dry breadcrumbs
1 pike (4–5 lb/2–2.2 kg), scaled and cleaned
1 egg, well beaten
2 tbsp (25 mL) butter, melted
Fresh lemon juice

Melt the butter in a saucepan over medium heat. Add the onion and cook for 1 minute. Stir in the oysters, parsley, salt, pepper, and mace. Cook for another minute. Remove from the heat and stir in the breadcrumbs.

Wash and dry pike thoroughly. If leaving the head on, remove the gills. Stir the egg into the oyster stuffing and stuff the pike. Close the opening with toothpicks or coarse thread. Place the fish in a greased roasting pan or large casserole and brush with the melted butter. Cover with foil and bake at 400°F (200°C) for 30 minutes or until cooked through (until the flesh releases easily from the bone). Serve immediately with lemon juice. ❦

Dancing Men Kedgeree

"We have let this affair go far enough," said he. "Is there a train to North Walsham tonight?"

I turned to the time-table. The last had just gone.

"Then we shall breakfast early and take the very first in the morning," said Holmes. "Our presence is most urgently needed ..."

THE ADVENTURE OF THE DANCING MEN

Kedgeree is traditionally a breakfast dish, easily fixed and substantial fare for anyone facing a rigorous and challenging day. A perfect choice for Mrs Hudson to put on the breakfast table as Holmes and Watson prepare to take an early train to Riding Thorpe Manor in Norfolk, where they will have to deal with the Chicago gangster Abe Slaney, murderer of their current client, Mr Hilton Cubbit.

This recipe calls for salmon, although a white-fleshed fish will do very well.

Serves 4

    3 tbsp (50 mL) butter
    6 cups (1.5 L) cooked long-grain rice
        (2 cups/500 mL raw)
    1 1/2 cups (375 mL) white sauce (béchamel)
        (see recipe on pages 182–183)

1 tbsp (15 mL) finely chopped fresh parsley
Salt and pepper
1 lb (500 g) cooked fish, skin and bones removed,
    and broken into bite-sized pieces
4 hard-boiled eggs, finely chopped

Melt the butter in a large saucepan over medium heat and stir in the rice. Stir in the white sauce, parsley, and salt and pepper to taste. Gently fold in the fish and eggs, taking care not to break the fish up any further. Transfer to a 12-cup (3 L) casserole dish and bake, covered, at 350°F (180°C) for 20 minutes or until the kedgeree is hot.

Note: Approximately 1 1/2 lbs (750 g) of fresh fish must be bought if 1 1b (500 g) of cooked fish is required. 🍎

Broiled Herring in Oatmeal

We had all listened with the deepest interest to this sketch of the night's doings, which Holmes had deduced from signs so subtle and minute that, even when he had pointed them out to us, we could scarcely follow him in his reasonings. The inspector hurried away on the instant to make inquiries ... while Holmes and I returned to Baker Street for breakfast.

THE ADVENTURE OF THE RESIDENT PATIENT

*H*olmes and Watson's breakfast came near the end of a strange case involving the murder of a bank robber turned informer named Blessington. Breakfasts at Baker Street often consisted of bacon and eggs, but in this case we have one of Mrs Hudson's Scottish favourites, Broiled Herring in Oatmeal. It goes very well with the mustard sauce recipe that follows.

Serves 4

> 4 fresh herring, cleaned
> 2 tsp (10 mL) salt
> 1/4 tsp (1 mL) pepper
> 1/3 cup (75 mL) quick-cooking oatmeal
> 1/4 cup (50 mL) butter

Wash the herring, making sure that the spinal vein along the backbone has been scraped out. Remove the head if desired. Score each fish diagonally three times on each side to expose the flesh and allow for even cooking. Sprinkle the inside of the fish with half of the salt.

Mix the remaining salt and the pepper with the oatmeal in a

shallow dish. Press both sides of each herring in the oatmeal. Lay on a baking sheet, top with small pats of half the butter, and broil on both sides for 5 minutes each, laying on pats of remaining butter when the fish are turned over. Serve with Mustard Sauce.

MUSTARD SAUCE

In addition to complementing herring, this sauce goes well with a variety of other fish, such as mackerel and poached cod.

Makes about 1 1/2 cups (375 mL)

> 2 tbsp (25 mL) butter
> 2 tbsp (25 mL) all-purpose flour
> 1 cup (250 mL) milk
> 1/4 cup (50 mL) whipping (35%) cream
> 2 tsp (10 mL) Dijon-style mustard
> 1 tsp (5 mL) white vinegar
> 1 tsp (5 mL) sugar
> 1 tsp (5 mL) salt
> 1/4 tsp (1 mL) pepper

Melt the butter in a saucepan over medium heat, then add the flour and cook, stirring, for 1 minute until it forms a smooth paste. Raise the heat and add the milk gradually, stirring continuously with a whisk until the sauce thickens. Reduce the heat and simmer, stirring, for 2 minutes. Stir in the cream, mustard, vinegar, sugar, salt, and pepper. Serve hot.

Note: The sauce must be thickened before the vinegar is added or it will curdle. ❦

Drambuie Baked Trout

"Is there good fishing in that part of Berkshire?"
"Well, sir, I've heard there are trout in the mill-stream ..."
"That's good enough. Watson and I are famous fishermen—are
we not, Watson?"

THE ADVENTURE OF SHOSCOMBE OLD PLACE

*H*olmes's fishing expedition was meant as a cover for his investigation of Sir Robert Norberton, a deeply indebted man who would stop at nothing to see that his horse won an important Derby. During their stay in Berkshire, Holmes and Watson likely caught both trout and pike, and perhaps they brought part of their catch back to Mrs Hudson.

Serves 4

> 4 speckled or rainbow trout, cleaned but with
>   their heads left on (approx. 1 lb/ 500 g each)
> 1/4 cup (50 mL) butter, softened
> 1 tsp (5 mL) dried tarragon
> 5 tbsp (75 mL) Drambuie
> 1 cup (250 mL) whipping (35%) cream
> 1 tsp (5 mL) salt
> 1 tbsp (15 mL) lemon zest

Wash the fish, then dry them completely. With half the butter, grease a baking dish just large enough to hold the fish. Arrange the fish in the baking dish; spread the remaining butter over them and sprinkle with tarragon.

Mix half the Drambuie with the cream and salt, then pour it over the trout. Bake, uncovered, at 350°F (180°C) for 20 minutes. Sprinkle with the rest of the Drambuie and the lemon zest before serving. ❧

Smoked Haddock
and Bacon Pie

It was a few weeks before my own marriage, during the days when I was still sharing rooms with Holmes in Baker Street, that he came home from an afternoon stroll to find a letter on the table waiting for him …

"Here is a very fashionable epistle," I remarked as he entered. "Your morning letters, if I remember right, were from a fish-monger and a tide-waiter."

THE ADVENTURE OF THE NOBLE BACHELOR

Why a fishmonger would have written to Holmes remains a matter of conjecture, but Mrs Hudson would have been quite familiar with the fishmongers near Baker Street, and one of her purchases from them would have been smoked haddock, reminiscent of the finnan haddock from her native Scotland. This dish goes well with a green salad and fresh rolls.

Serves 4

> 8 slices bacon
> 3 tbsp (50 mL) butter
> 2 lb (1 kg) smoked haddock fillets, skin removed
> 2 tomatoes, sliced
> 1 cup (250 mL) dry breadcrumbs

Cut the bacon into 2-inch (5 cm) pieces and fry it until brown but not crisp. Drain and set aside. Grease a deep 8-inch (20 cm) pie plate with 1 tbsp (15 mL) of the butter. Flake the haddock, removing any bones, and put it in the pie plate. Spread the tomatoes over it and lay on the bacon. Sprinkle breadcrumbs evenly on top and dot with the remaining butter. Bake at 350°F (180°C) for 20 minutes. Serve immediately. 🐾

Hot Pickled Salmon

It was a wild, tempestuous night towards the close of November. Holmes and I sat together in silence all the evening ... Outside the wind howled down Baker Street, while the rain beat fiercely against the windows.

THE ADVENTURE OF THE GOLDEN PINCE-NEZ

As the London weather grew cold and bitter, Mrs Hudson would have drawn from her stock of recipes those most suitable for winter weather.

Serves 4

> 2-lb (1 kg) piece fresh salmon
> 1 tsp (5 mL) salt
> 1 cup (250 mL) medium-dry white wine
> 2 tsp (10 mL) grated fresh ginger
> 10 peppercorns
> 6 whole cloves
> 2 tsp (10 mL) sugar
> 1/2 tsp (2 mL) mace
> 2 tbsp (25 mL) chopped fresh parsley

Put the salmon into a nonreactive saucepan and add water to cover. Add salt, bring to a boil, then lower heat, cover, and simmer for 20 minutes or until the flesh just begins to separate from the bone.

Carefully remove the salmon; discard any skin. Stir the wine, ginger, peppercorns, cloves, sugar, and mace into the warm stock. Return the fish to the stock and let it marinate overnight in the refrigerator. Reheat the fish in the marinade until it is just hot enough to serve (3–5 minutes). Be careful not to overcook. Carefully remove from the marinade and garnish with parsley. 🍎

Smoked Salmon and
Parsley Pâté

Sherlock Holmes was pacing up and down the platform, his tall, gaunt figure made even gaunter and taller by his long grey travelling-cloak and close-fitting cloth cap.

"It is very good of you to come, Watson," said he. "It makes a considerable difference to me, having someone with me on whom I can thoroughly rely … If you will keep the two corner seats I shall get the tickets."

THE BOSCOMBE VALLEY MYSTERY

*H*olmes and Watson travelled by train all over England. These frequent trips always demanded nourishment, and train fare was notoriously bad. It would have been up to Mrs Hudson to provide food for their journeys, and sandwiches filled with a smoked salmon pâté would have been greatly appreciated.

Makes 4 sandwiches

> 1/2 lb (250 g) smoked salmon
> 2/3 cup (150 mL) chopped fresh parsley
> 1/3 cup (75 mL) whipping (35%) cream
> 1/4 cup (50 mL) butter, softened
> 1 tbsp (15 mL) lime juice
> 1 tsp (5 mL) sugar
> 1/2 tsp (2 mL) salt
> 1/4 tsp (1 mL) pepper
> 1/4 tsp (1 mL) nutmeg

Remove any small bones from the salmon. In a food processor, purée the salmon with the parsley, cream, butter, lime juice, sugar, salt, pepper, and nutmeg. Put the mixture into a small bowl and chill until needed. 🐾

Deep-Fried Scallops with Bacon

During my long and intimate acquaintance with Mr Sherlock Holmes I had
never heard him refer to his relations, and hardly ever to his own early life.

THE ADVENTURE OF THE GREEK INTERPRETER

*H*olmes did reveal that his ancestors were of the country squire class, and some Sherlockians believe that he was from Yorkshire. If so, we can assume that he was familiar with traditional Yorkshire high tea dishes, such as this one.

Serves 4

8 slices lean bacon
3 eggs
1/4 tsp (1 mL) pepper
2 tbsp (25 mL) all-purpose flour
1 1/2 cups (375 mL) fresh fine white breadcrumbs
Vegetable oil for deep-frying
2 lb (1 kg) scallops
1/4 cup (50 mL) chopped fresh parsley

Fry the bacon in a frying pan until crisp. Drain and chop it into bite-sized pieces. Keep warm.

In a small bowl beat together the eggs and pepper. Have ready in two separate dishes the flour and breadcrumbs.

Heat 3–4 inches (8–10 cm) of oil to 400°F (200°C) in a deep-fryer. Dust the scallops with the flour. Dip them in the egg, letting the excess drip off, then roll them in the breadcrumbs. Deep-fry the scallops for 3 minutes. Drain on paper towels.

Arrange scallops on plates, scatter the bacon over the scallops, sprinkle with parsley, and serve immediately. ❦

Poultry and Game

One of the largest stalls bore the name of Breckinridge upon it, and the proprietor, a horsy-looking man, with a sharp face and trim side-whiskers, was helping a boy to put up the shutters.

"Good evening. It's a cold night," said Holmes.

The salesman nodded, and shot a questioning glance at my companion.

"Sold out of geese, I see," continued Holmes, pointing at the bare slabs of marble.

"Let you have five hundred tomorrow morning."

THE ADVENTURE OF THE BLUE CARBUNCLE

olmes's conversation with the poulterer Breckinridge eventually furnished him with an address in East London where a local woman fattened geese for sale. They were "town-bred" geese, although many of the thousands of geese that arrived at Covent Garden were "country-bred" and were brought in by rail. In earlier years the birds walked; immense flocks of hissing geese and gobbling turkeys from as far away as Lincolnshire, Cambridge, Suffolk, and Norfolk set out near the end of August like huge gangs of convicts on a fated three-month tramp to the unhappy terminus of the London markets. Other regular poultry arrivals in London were ducks from the Aylesbury district and Surrey chickens, the latter having been on a several-week, round-the-clock fattening plan, with night candles burning in their coops and their feeding troughs piled high with raisins and corn soaked in milk.

Caesar noted that the early Britons kept geese and hens for pleasure, but that there was a religious taboo on eating them. This circumstance changed with the Roman occupiers, who were happy to eat ducks, pigeons, pheasants, and the ancestor of all domestic chickens, the Red Jungle Fowl of India, which had travelled to Rome via Persia and Greece and arrived in Britain with the legions. Both the Romans and their British subjects ate such wild birds as cranes, pelicans, herons, larks, sparrows, and thrushes. The larger birds were killed with arrows or trapped in snares and the smaller ones were caught with fine nets.

Falconry, a more efficient method of catching wildfowl, was introduced in the ninth century and enjoyed widespread popularity with the gentry after the Norman Conquest. The upper orders held a monopoly on the bigger killing birds such as the peregrine falcon, and set them on herons, bitterns, and other large fowl, while the lesser hawks of the common people took such birds as the partridge, and were also used in the "daring of larks," an activity in which a small falcon was employed to petrify larks flightless while fowlers caught them easily with nets on the ground.

Poultry dealing was recognized early as a trade, and the Company of Poulters was in existence in London by the end of the thirteenth century in an area given the not unlikely name of The Poultry. The birds of choice gradually changed over the years. By the late 1700s cranes and herons, as well as the formerly much sought after and expensive cygnet (young swan), had lost their appeal, while the "bustard," a large, flightless, fast-running bird that was hunted with greyhounds, was extinct. Also, many of the smaller birds, such as robins, finches, and thrushes, had been dropped from the menu. Doves were still eaten, and pigeon was a common meat all through the Victorian era, as is evidenced by the number of pigeon recipes in the cookbooks of the day. However, the turkey, which was originally from Mexico and Central America and introduced into England in the mid-sixteenth century, became very popular. By Holmes's day it was beginning to mount a challenge to the goose as the bird most favoured as Christmas fare.

Like falconry, the pursuit of wild game was always largely a pastime of the nobility in Britain, even during the pre-Roman Iron Age. Red and roe deer, bear, wild oxen, boars, and even horses were caught and eaten. The Saxon aristocracy hunted game in enclosed parks, of which the *Domesday Book* lists thirty-one in the lowland area of Britain alone. The Normans enforced personal ownership of all forest lands and game. These strictures were later relaxed and the aristocracy hunted in their own large enclosures, while villagers were allowed to hunt hares, rabbits, and boars in other areas of the forest. Deer, however, remained the prerogative of the landowners; venison was not sold on the open market and severe penalties were handed out to those who poached it.

In 1846 the Corn Laws, which for generations had restricted grain imports to England, were repealed and the prices of domestic wheat and other cereals dropped dramatically, seriously threatening the prosperity and lifestyle of the property-owning classes. However, the attraction of the life of the landed gentry remained undimmed, and the rising tide of newly rich industrialists were quick to acquire the estates and such traditional customs of the squirarchy as hunting. It wasn't long before the annual August grouse shoot, involving beaters, hunters, shotgun loaders, well-trained spaniels, and thousands of doomed birds, was a social event on a par with the Ascot races.

"My ancestors were country squires, who appear to have led much the same life as is natural to their class," Holmes says in *The Adventure of the Greek Interpreter*, revealing that in his own background he was acquainted with the hunting and shooting habits of leisured country society. Both he and Watson would have also appreciated the game cookery of their day, both through the efforts of Mrs Hudson and at the tables of the many titled and well-to-do individuals with country estates who found themselves in need of his services. ❦

Quail on Toast

"I am somewhat of a fowl fancier ..."

THE ADVENTURE OF THE BLUE CARBUNCLE

*H*olmes made this remark to Henry Baker, a man whose stolen goose became the centrepiece of an investigation into a precious-gem robbery. Holmes was quite familiar with a variety of fowl, particularly game birds. He probably hunted for them in his youth, and frequently ate them at Baker Street and in other surroundings. Quail is one of the favourite and more easily cooked of Victorian game birds.

Serves 4 as an appetizer

> 4 quails
> 1/4 cup (50 mL) butter
> 2 tbsp (25 mL) finely chopped fresh parsley
> 1/2 tsp (2 mL) salt
> 4 slices lean bacon
> 8 slices toast, crusts removed

Rinse the quails inside and out and wipe them dry. Divide 1 tbsp (15 mL) of the butter evenly among the birds, putting a small pat inside each cavity, along with a quarter of the parsley and a sprinkling of salt. Wrap a slice of bacon around each quail and secure it with a toothpick.

Melt the remaining butter in a heavy frying pan over medium heat and fry the quails until they are completely cooked, turning to brown all sides (about 20–25 minutes). Remove from the pan and with a sharp knife cut each quail in half through the breastbone. Spoon about a teaspoon of the pan drippings on each piece of toast and lay half of a quail, leg side up, on top of the toast. 🐦

Braised Haunch of Venison with Port Wine

It was a very large and high chamber, with carved oak ceiling, oaken panelling, and a fine array of deer's heads and ancient weapons around the walls.

THE ADVENTURE OF THE ABBEY GRANGE

Watson is describing the dining room of the Abbey Grange, a large property of the late Sir Eustace Brackenstall, one of the richest men in Kent. The deer heads may well have come from a herd kept in the large park surrounding the house noted by the doctor on his way in. Venison would have long been popular on an estate such as the Abbey Grange, as it would have in the numerous great country houses Holmes visited in his professional capacity. It was probably served to them on many occasions.

Venison can be a dry meat, requiring constant basting if roasted. This recipe allows the meat to retain its moisture. Venison is usually hung for seven to ten days in a cool place to improve its flavour before it is cooked. Store-bought venison has normally been hung for the required period.

Serves 4–6

2–3 tbsp (25–50 mL) unsalted butter or cooking oil
1 (2–3 lb/1–1.5 kg) boned haunch (loin) of venison
2 medium onions, chopped
6 slices lean bacon, chopped
1 1/2 cups (375 mL) port
1 cup (250 mL) cranberries
1 tsp (5 mL) cinnamon
1 tsp (5 mL) salt
1/2 tsp (2 mL) pepper
1–2 cups (250–500 mL) (approx.) beef stock

Melt the butter over medium-high heat in a large ovenproof saucepan. Brown the venison all over and set it aside. Add the onions and bacon to the pot and fry for 3–4 minutes, stirring, until the onions are beginning to be transparent. Stir in the port, cranberries, cinnamon, salt, and pepper. Return the venison to the pot.

Add enough stock to come halfway up the meat. Bring to a boil. Remove from the heat and cover tightly, using foil if necessary, to prevent loss of moisture. Bake at 325°F (160°C) for 2 hours, or until the meat is tender. Remove the meat to a warm platter and keep it warm.

Boil the cooking liquid over medium-high heat, stirring it continuously until it begins to thicken. Adjust seasoning. Pour the sauce over the meat.

Serve the venison with potatoes and a green vegetable. 🦃

Game Pie

"I have oysters and a brace of grouse, with something a little choice in white wine.—Watson, you have never recognized my merits as a housekeeper."

THE SIGN OF FOUR

*H*olmes's brace of grouse were no doubt prepared and cooked by Mrs Hudson. Her own experience was probably more with the red grouse of the Scottish moors, although the birds her famous lodger had acquired were likely white grouse, or ptarmigan. Mrs Hudson may have roasted them, but she might well have put them in a game pie recipe similar to this one.

Store-bought grouse has normally been hung. If not, then the indoor hanging period is two to four days.

Serves 4–6

1/2 cup (125 mL) red wine
1/3 cup (75 mL) red currant jelly
1 tsp (5 mL) nutmeg
1/2 tsp (2 mL) cloves
1 lb (500 g) grouse or partridge, cut into
    1-inch (2.5 cm) pieces
1 lb (500 g) rabbit or hare, cut into 1-inch (2.5 cm) pieces
8 slices lean bacon
1 cup (250 mL) roughly chopped mushrooms

1 tsp (5 mL) savory
1 tsp (5 mL) marjoram
1 tsp (5 mL) salt
1/4 tsp (1 mL) pepper
1/4-lb (125 g) ham steak, cut into 1/2-inch (1 cm) fingers
1/2 cup (125 mL) chicken stock
Puff pastry for one 9-inch (23 cm) pie crust
1 egg beaten with 1 tbsp (15 mL) milk

Heat the wine in a saucepan until it simmers; stir in the red currant jelly until it is dissolved. Add the nutmeg and cloves. Pour the mixture into a bowl; add the grouse and rabbit pieces and marinate them in the refrigerator for 1 hour, stirring occasionally to make sure all the meat is marinated.

Lay the bacon slices in a round casserole or baking dish that is at least 2 inches (5 cm) deep. Layer half the game pieces on top of the bacon along with half of the marinade. Sprinkle half of the mushrooms, savory, marjoram, salt, and pepper on top. Then lay in the ham fingers. Add the rest of the game and marinade, and then the rest of the mushrooms and spices. Pour in the chicken stock.

On a lightly floured surface, roll out the pastry to cover the dish and unfold it over the pie. Trim off the excess pastry and crimp the edges to be sure that the pie is tightly sealed. Gather the pastry scraps into a ball, roll it out, and cut out a few simple flower or leaf shapes. Moisten one side of these with a little of the egg mixture and arrange on the pie. Brush all the pastry with the remaining egg mixture and cut a 1-inch (2.5 cm) hole in the centre to let out steam.

Bake at 400°F (200°C) for 20 minutes. Reduce heat to 350°F (180°C) and bake for 1 hour or until golden brown. Serve directly from the baking dish. 🦃

"Gloria Scott" Duck

*"Old Trevor was evidently a man of some wealth and consideration,
a J.P., and a landed proprietor. Donnithorpe is a little hamlet just
to the north of Langmere, in the country of the Broads. The house
was an old-fashioned, widespread, oak-beamed brick building,
with a fine lime-lined avenue leading up to it. There was excellent
wild-duck shooting in the fens …"*

THE ADVENTURE OF THE "GLORIA SCOTT"

The "Gloria Scott" affair was Holmes's first case, undertaken
while vacationing at the home of Victor Trevor, a friend from
his university years. It is quite probable that he went duck
hunting during his stay, and whatever he bagged would have
found its way onto the Trevor family dinner table.

One of the difficulties with the usual supermarket duck is its
fat content and the amount of grease involved when it is cooked.
This recipe, adapted from Mrs Beeton's *Book of Household
Management* (1861), eliminates much of that problem.

Serves 3

1 (4–5 lb/2–2.2 kg) duck
2 tsp (10 mL) salt
2 medium onions, sliced
1 tbsp (15 mL) oil or butter
1 1/2 tsp (7 mL) dried thyme
1 tsp (5 mL) dried sage
1/4 tsp (1 mL) pepper
2 tsp (10 mL) lemon juice
6 cups (1.5 L) beef stock
1 tsp (5 mL) cornstarch

Wash the duck, dry it well, then rub it inside and out with 1 tsp (5 mL) of the salt. Pierce the skin all over, but not deeply enough to penetrate the flesh. Roast the duck on a rack in a roasting pan at 425°F (220°C) for 30 minutes.

Meanwhile, in a large pot, fry the onions lightly in the oil. Stir in the thyme, sage, pepper, remaining salt, and lemon juice.

Remove the duck from the oven and wipe off excess grease with paper towels. Put it in the pot with the onions; add the beef stock. Bring to a boil, then reduce the heat and simmer until the duck is tender (45–60 minutes).

Remove the duck from the pot, cover with foil, and keep it warm in the oven. Pour the stock into a bowl and refrigerate it for 30 minutes to help the fat rise to the surface. Skim off the fat. In a small saucepan, reheat 1 cup (250 mL) of the stock. Stir together the cornstarch and 1 tbsp (15 mL) of cold water. Stir into stock until thickened slightly. Adjust seasoning, then pour over the duck and serve. ❦

Naval Treaty
Chicken Curry

"Mrs Hudson has risen to the occasion," said Holmes, uncovering a dish of curried chicken ... "What have you there, Watson?"

"Ham and eggs," I answered.

"Good! What are you going to take, Mr. Phelps—curried fowl, eggs, or will you help yourself?"

"Thank you, I can eat nothing," said Phelps.

THE ADVENTURE OF THE NAVAL TREATY

*P*ercy "Tadpole" Phelps was an old school friend of Dr Watson's who came to Holmes for help in finding the stolen text of an important naval treaty between England and Italy. Near the end of the case he was invited to Baker Street for breakfast, but his anxiety over the missing treaty dominated any pangs of hunger he would have usually felt. The contemporary reader might find the prospect of curried chicken itself somewhat of an appetite suppressant in the early hours of the morning. But the Victorian digestive constitution was normally very robust, and there were often dishes set on the table that stretched the definition of a "hearty breakfast."

This chicken curry will probably be most successfully served as part of an evening meal. Unlike some curry dishes of the day, which involved mixing curry pastes with reheated cold chicken, the flavour of this recipe is greatly enhanced by beginning with a whole chicken. This curry goes well with basmati rice and a green salad.

Serves 3–4

1 (3 lb/1.5 kg) chicken
1 tsp (5 mL) salt
2 tbsp (25 mL) cornstarch
3 tbsp (50 mL) unsalted butter
3 onions, sliced
4 cloves garlic, minced
2 tsp (10 mL) ground coriander
1 tsp (5 mL) mustard seeds
1 tsp (5 mL) cumin
1 tsp (5 mL) turmeric
1 tsp (5 mL) ginger
2 cups (500 mL) unsweetened coconut milk
2 tsp (10 mL) lime juice
Salt and pepper to taste

Joint the chicken and remove the skin. Cut chicken into pieces no larger than 2 inches (5 cm) with a cleaver or heavy kitchen knife. Sprinkle them with salt and dust with cornstarch. Melt the butter in a large saucepan over medium heat and brown the chicken pieces. Remove from the pan and set them aside.

Add the onion and garlic to the saucepan and sauté, stirring, for 2 minutes. Add the coriander, mustard seeds, cumin, turmeric, and ginger; cook, stirring, for 2 more minutes. Return the chicken to the saucepan and cook for 5 minutes, stirring to make sure all pieces are coated well with spices. Add the coconut milk. Simmer, uncovered, for 30 minutes or until the chicken is cooked through and tender. Stir in the lime juice and season with salt and pepper.

Note: If a cleaver or heavy kitchen knife is not available, this recipe may be made with ready-cut pieces of chicken (drumsticks, breasts, wings, etc.). The simmering time will be longer. 🐝

Pheasant in Cream Sauce
with Brandy

"I have to keep up a considerable staff of servants at Hurlstone, for it is a rambling old place, and takes a good deal of looking after. I preserve, too, and in the pheasant months I usually have a house party, so that it would not do to be short-handed."

THE ADVENTURE OF THE MUSGRAVE RITUAL

These comments are made by Reginald Musgrave, an acquaintance of Holmes's from his undergraduate days. Musgrave's house party during the pheasant season, which opened on the first of October, was not an unusual event for someone in his position.

The pheasant was the king of game birds in Victorian society and was not a regular feature of Holmes's or Watson's diet. It is something they might have eaten when visiting someone like Musgrave or in the Diogenes Club frequented by Holmes's brother, Mycroft, although Mrs Hudson may have occasionally ordered pheasant from her butcher when they were in season.

Regulations prohibit the sale of pheasants in some places, but when it is possible to purchase them, they are often bought in a brace (a cock and a hen). The cock is a drier bird and has less flavour than a hen. It is also common to hang game birds, particularly partridge and grouse, for three to ten days to enhance their flavour and tenderize their meat. This may not be entirely desirable in the home of the contemporary cook. However, most game birds bought in a supermarket have usually been hung for the desired period.

This dish goes well with rice and a green vegetable.

Serves 4

> 3 tbsp (50 mL) unsalted butter
> 2 lb (1 kg) pheasant pieces (meat from 2 birds)
> 3/4 cup (175 mL) apple juice
> 1 tsp (5 mL) salt
> 1 cup (250 mL) whipping (35%) cream
> 3 tbsp (50 mL) brandy
> 2 tbsp (25 mL) all-purpose flour
> 2 tbsp (25 mL) butter, softened
> 2 turns of pepper from a pepper mill
>   (or 1/2 tsp/2 mL ground pepper)

In a large saucepan, melt the butter over medium heat and brown the pheasant pieces. Add the apple juice and salt, cover, and simmer over low heat for 30 minutes or until pheasant is tender, adding more juice if necessary. Remove the pheasant pieces and set aside. Add the cream and brandy to the pan and heat until boiling. Meanwhile, blend the flour with the softened butter to make a *beurre manié*. Add this bit by bit to the boiling cream, whisking until the mixture thickens enough to coat the back of a spoon. Stir in the pheasant pieces and heat through. Stir in the pepper and serve immediately.

Note: Additional cream may be used as an alternative to flour and butter as a thickener. Add another cup (250 mL) of cream and cook until it thickens to the desired consistency. 🍎

Rabbit with
Red Currant Jelly

"I then took my gun and strolled out in the direction of the Boscombe Pool, with the intention of visiting the rabbit-warren which is on the other side. On the way I saw William Crowder, the gamekeeper ..."

THE BOSCOMBE VALLEY MYSTERY

The Boscombe Valley in this adventure was in Herefordshire, and the rabbit-warren mentioned was on the considerable property of John Turner, an ex-Australian who was a key figure in Holmes's investigation of a murder nearby.

Rabbits were a popular meat with the Victorians. They were cheap and plentiful, often making a nuisance of themselves in gardens. Unlike hares, they do not have to be hung, but can be eaten fresh. This particular recipe originates in Scotland, where rabbits have always been more of a Lowland than a Highland fare. It is very likely that Mrs Hudson prepared rabbit in this fashion.

Serves 3–4

1 (4–5 lb/2–2.2 kg) rabbit, cut into serving pieces
1 cup (250 mL) all-purpose flour, seasoned with
    1/2 tsp (2 mL) salt and 1/4 tsp (1 mL) pepper
2–3 tbsp (25–50 mL) unsalted butter or cooking oil
2 medium onions, chopped
8 slices lean bacon, chopped
1 cup (250 mL) chopped mushrooms
1/4 cup (50 mL) chopped fresh parsley
1 tsp (5 mL) allspice
1 tsp (5 mL) salt
1/4 tsp (1 mL) pepper
1/4 cup (50 mL) red wine
3 cups (750 mL) beef stock
3 tbsp (50 mL) red currant jelly
1–2 tbsp (25–50 mL) cornstarch (optional)

Dust the rabbit pieces with the seasoned flour and brown in a large saucepan in 2 tbsp (25 mL) of butter over medium heat. Remove and set aside.

Add the remaining butter to the pan if necessary and fry the onions and bacon, stirring, for 1 minute. Add the mushrooms, parsley, allspice, salt, and pepper. Cook for another minute. Add the rabbit pieces and stir well to coat them with the spices. Add the wine and beef stock, bring to a boil, then simmer, covered, for 1 1/2 hours or until the rabbit is tender.

Transfer the rabbit pieces to a warm platter and keep warm. Skim the sauce and strain it. Reheat it and stir in the red currant jelly. Adjust the seasoning. If the sauce is too thin, dissolve the cornstarch in 1 tbsp (15 mL) cold water and stir it in. Pour the sauce over the rabbit and serve immediately. ❦

Meat

"Thank you, Watson, you must help me on with my coat. When we have finished at the police-station I think that something nutritious at Simpson's would not be out of place."

THE ADVENTURE OF THE DYING DETECTIVE

t is understandable that Holmes's thoughts turned to food as he wound up this case. It had demanded he undergo a three-day fast to alter his appearance and deceive Culverton Smith, a murderous planter from Sumatra with a knowledge of rare tropical diseases that he used to homicidal effect. The Simpson's Holmes is referring to is Simpson's-in-the-Strand, which opened in 1848, was rebuilt in 1904, and to this day is particularly famous for its roast beef, which is likely what he had in mind when he suggested something nutritious.

Beef held an unchallenged pride of place as the national dish in the Victorian era, and the "roast beef of olde England" was as much of a cherished symbol of Britain as John Bull in his Union Jack waistcoat, although both were notions that really only came into prominence in the eighteenth century—John Bull being a figure of the patriotic squirarchy, and the year-round availability of beef the result of agricultural innovations during the same period. As Holmes himself came from a country squire background, and Watson's family history was well-to-do middle class, both men would expect to see beef regularly set before them whether in Baker Street or "superior places of refreshment," such as Simpson's, the Criterion Hotel in Piccadilly, Mycroft Holmes's Diogenes Club in Pall Mall, the Café Royal in Regent Street (another great favourite with Holmes), or even in the chop-houses they would have frequented in the more impecunious, earlier days of their association.

Historically, quite a wide variety of flesh-bearing animals, such as deer, horses, wild pigs, hares, and even squirrels, were killed and eaten in Britain with great enthusiasm. The meat was roasted warm from the kill or hung until it was tender. Little of the animal was wasted—the bones were broken for their marrow, and the gut was used as a sausage casing in which to cook the internal organs. As the years passed an ambivalent attitude was taken to the offal of animals. In the Middle Ages, for example, the "umbles," or internal organs of deer, were highly regarded, but by the Tudor period they were looked upon as an inferior food, and the expression "to eat umble-pie" evoked the sense of offal as a repugnant food eaten only by the poverty stricken. Victorian cookery books do contain some recipes for items such as liver, brains, and calf's head, but given the antecedents of both Holmes and Watson, dishes such as tripe and onions, for example, probably held little attraction for them, although they may have enjoyed a good beef steak and kidney pudding.

During Anglo-Saxon times, the pig was an important animal, particularly among the poor, but in the years following the Norman invasion the numbers of cattle increased and sheep and goat farming was expanded. The pig was not neglected, however, and during the medieval period two British pork-related specialties were developed. One was collops (rashers) of bacon fried with eggs, and the other was the rich and fatty dish of brawn, made from the foreparts and head of a boar or pig. This was considered a delicacy at a medieval feast, became fare during the twelve days of Christmas in the Tudor age, and is still mentioned in Victorian Christmas menus.

Goat meat gradually went out of fashion after the Middle Ages, but the quality of other livestock improved with new feed grasses from Europe and the large enclosures of common land that gave landowners greater space in which to nurture their animals. Cattle brought in from Holland and pigs from China strengthened the native stock, and by the late eighteenth century English beef, mutton, and pork were becoming the envy of Europe. Improvements in winter feeding meant there was less need for the enormous autumn slaughters of earlier years, and roasted meat sauces became simpler as the better quality of the meat rendered the more pungent flavourings of former days unnecessary. The enormous meat pies common to the Middle Ages also became less elaborate; many of the rich, sweet fruits and spices were removed, leaving a more subtle and savoury taste.

By the nineteenth century, refrigeration and canning processes brought meat from America, the Argentine, Australia, and New Zealand. The railroads carried sheep from Wales, pigs from Ireland, Aberdeen Angus from Scotland, and the best beef of England to meat markets such as Smithfield in London and its equivalent in other growing urban centres. In *The Adventure of the Engineer's Thumb*, a railway station-master comments of a thin man that "he looks as if a little good Berkshire beef would do him no harm," a prescription with which Dr Watson and Holmes would no doubt heartily agree. 🍂

Devil's Foot Cornish Pasties

Thus it was that in the early spring of that year we found ourselves together in a small cottage near Poldhu Bay, at the further extremity of the Cornish peninsula.

THE ADVENTURE OF THE DEVIL'S FOOT

*H*olmes and Watson were in Cornwall more than once. On this occasion they have taken up residence there on the advice of Dr Agar of Harley Street, whose concern for the Great Detective's health prompted him to suggest "a complete change of scene and air" away from the demands of work. Holmes contented himself with a study of the Cornish language and solitary walks on the surrounding moors until their vacation was interrupted by a demand for him to solve a local mystery. However, during their stay we can be assured that they became familiar with the local cuisine. The Cornish pasty has its origins as the tin miner's lunch, and its portability would have appealed to Holmes on his countryside walks.

Makes 4 7-inch (18 cm) pasties

PASTRY
2 cups (500 mL) all-purpose flour
1/2 tsp (2 mL) salt
3/4 cup (175 mL) shortening
4–5 tbsp (50–75 mL) ice water

Combine the flour and salt. Cut in the shortening until crumbly. Stir in 4 tbsp (50 mL) ice water to form a ball. If the dough crumbles, add the remaining water. Refrigerate for at least 1 hour.

FILLING
1 lb (500 g) lean beef, diced
1 cup (250 mL) diced potatoes
1/2 cup (125 mL) chopped onions
1/2 cup (125 mL) diced turnip
1/2 cup (125 mL) thinly sliced carrots
1 1/2 tsp (7 mL) salt
1 tsp (5 mL) pepper
1 tsp (5 mL) savory
1 tbsp (15 mL) tomato ketchup
1 tsp (5 mL) Worcestershire sauce
1 egg, lightly beaten

Roll out the dough on a lightly floured surface and with a pastry wheel or a sharp knife cut it into four 7-inch (18 cm) rounds. In a bowl mix together the beef, potatoes, onions, turnip, carrots, salt, pepper, savory, ketchup, and Worcestershire sauce. Moisten edges of pastry rounds with cold water. Place one-quarter of mixture in the centre of each round, fold over completely, and crimp edges to seal.

Place the pasties on a baking sheet and cut two 1-inch (2.5 cm) slits on the top of each. Brush with beaten egg and bake at 400°F (200°C) for 15 minutes. Reduce heat to 350°F (180°C) and bake for another 30 minutes or until pastry is golden. Serve hot or at room temperature. 🍎

Illustrious Client
Roast Beef and
Yorkshire Pudding

It was not possible for me to follow the immediate steps taken by my friend, for I had some pressing professional business of my own, but I met him by appointment that evening at Simpson's, where, sitting at a small table in the front window, and looking down at the rushing stream of life in the Strand, he told me something of what had passed.

THE ADVENTURE OF THE ILLUSTRIOUS CLIENT

*I*t was no doubt over Simpson's famous roast beef and Yorkshire pudding that Holmes told Watson of his plans to thwart the marriage of the murderous philanderer Baron Adelbert Grunner to the naive Miss Violet de Merville, an undertaking that almost cost the Great Detective his life. Simpson's was "our restaurant" in Watson's mind, and they must have reviewed many investigations at its tables.

Serves 6

1 (5 lb/2.2 kg) rib roast of beef

YORKSHIRE PUDDING

1/4 cup (50 mL) hot beef drippings
2 eggs
1/4 tsp (1 mL) salt
1 cup (250 mL) milk
1 1/4 cups (300 mL) all-purpose flour

Place the beef in a roasting pan, fat side up, using the ribs as a rack. Roast in the middle of the oven at 450°F (230°C) for 20 minutes. Reduce the heat to 325°F (160°C) and continue to roast until the meat is cooked. Allow a total of 27 minutes per pound for rare, 34 minutes for medium, and 41 for well done. Do not cover the meat, add water, or baste it. Transfer the beef to a heated platter and cover with foil to keep warm.

Pour a bit of the drippings into 6 muffin tins. Put the muffin pan in the middle of the oven and turn the oven up to 400°F (200°C). Beat together the eggs, salt, and milk, then slowly add the flour, beating until the batter is smooth. Pour the batter into the hot tins. Bake for 15 minutes, or until the puddings have risen and are beginning to brown. Reduce the heat to 350°F (180°C) and bake for another 10 minutes. Serve with the roast beef. 🐦

Inspector Lestrade's Favourite Toad-in-the-Hole

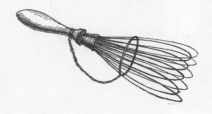

There was one little sallow, rat-faced, dark-eyed fellow who was introduced to me as Mr Lestrade, and who came three or four times in a single week.

A STUDY IN SCARLET

Watson first made the acquaintance of Inspector Lestrade of Scotland Yard in very early Baker Street days and noted that he appeared in their sitting room four times in the first week after he and Holmes had moved in together. Although Lestrade's dull and sometimes inept detective efforts were always dimmed by the brilliance of Holmes, he was no doubt a diligent and hard-working police officer, and probably deserved more than the meagre police salary he was paid. He would never have experienced the finer cuisine offered to Holmes and Watson in the great country houses and splendid London homes they visited.

Inspector Lestrade's Favourite Toad-in-the-Hole sounds as if it could refer to one of the more seedy London informants he might have kept on his books. However, the origins of toad-in-the-hole are found in an old recipe called *froise*, which involved deep-frying slices of bacon in batter. Later it became an inexpensive way of spreading a small amount of beef steak around a family, and on occasions when she was caught short for meat Mrs Hudson might have offered it to her lodgers. These days it is usually made with sausages.

Serves 4

> 2 eggs
> 1 cup (250 mL) milk
> 1/2 tsp (2 mL) salt
> 1/4 tsp (1 mL) pepper
> 1 1/4 cups (300 mL) all-purpose flour
> 1 lb (500 g) pork sausages
> 2 tbsp (25 mL) water

Beat the eggs with the milk, salt, and pepper in a bowl. Add the flour slowly, beating until the mixture is smooth and creamy.

Prick each sausage two or three times with a fork and lay them in a saucepan. Add the water, cover, and cook over low heat for 4 minutes. Remove the cover, increase the heat to medium and continue to cook, turning the sausages frequently, until they are brown on all sides.

Pat the sausages dry and place them in a single layer and 1- inch (2.5 cm) apart in a greased casserole dish. Pour the batter over them. Bake at 400°F (200°C) for 30 minutes or until the batter has risen and is crisp and brown. Serve immediately. ❦

Lamb Chops with Ginger/Lime Sauce

"Billy, you will show his lordship out, and tell Mrs Hudson that I should be glad if she would send up dinner for two as soon as possible."

THE ADVENTURE OF THE MAZARIN STONE

*H*olmes's dinner instructions come at the end of a trying investigation, but they are not as off the cuff as they might at first sound. Meal arrangements with Mrs Hudson were made near the beginning of this case, and as Dr Watson was not a lodger at Baker Street at this time, but came by only now and then to help the famous detective with his investigations, we can expect that she cooked something a little special for the occasion.

Scottish lamb of the sort Mrs Hudson would have been familiar with is a tender and well-loved meat, particularly the spring (three-to-five-month-old) variety. In Holmes's day the advent of freezing techniques and refrigeration chambers aboard cargo vessels meant that Argentinean, American, and Australian meats were being regularly unloaded at London docks. Consequently, she might have served young lamb chops at any time of the year.

The chops used in this recipe are also known as gigot chops. They are about 1-inch (2.5 cm) thick and have the bone in the centre of the meat. You may need to have them specially cut for you by your butcher.

It is best to remove as much fat as possible from lamb, as it is indigestible, and it is also wise to trim off the white membrane around the meat known as the fell. It can give the meat a strong flavour when cooked.

Serves 4

4 lamb leg chops
1 tsp (5 mL) salt
1 inch (2.5 cm) fresh ginger, grated
3 tbsp (50 mL) brown sugar
2 tbsp (25 mL) lime juice

Rub both sides of chops with salt and place in a buttered baking dish just large enough to hold them. Sprinkle with grated ginger and brown sugar, then pour lime juice over them. Let them sit in a cool place for an hour.

Cover and bake at 350°F (180°C) for 45 minutes. 🐦

Lancashire Hot Pot

"This northern air is invigorating and pleasant, so I propose to spend a few days upon your moors, and to occupy my mind as best I may. Whether I have the shelter of your roof or of the village inn is, of course, for you to decide." ...

"Far from going to the inn, Mr Holmes, I should be pleased if you would come and stay with me at Holdernesse Hall."

THE ADVENTURE OF THE PRIORY SCHOOL

*H*olmes found it useful to stay in Holdernesse Hall, located in the north of England, as he undertook to discover the whereabouts of the son of the Duke of Holdernesse, who had been abducted from the select preparatory school, The Priory. Both he and Watson undoubtedly fared well at the Hall, but had they stayed in less elevated surroundings they might have dined on Lancashire hot pot, a hearty casserole dish. Holmes would have already known of it through his own early years in northern England.

Originally a dish for workers in the Lancashire mills of the early days of the Industrial Revolution, Lancashire hot pot has always been characterized by a basic combination of lamb, onions, potatoes, and oysters. The lamb was usually of a cheaper cut, oysters were added because they were plentiful at that time, and the dish was cooked in an earthenware pot and served with pickled cabbage.

Serves 4

8 chops from the neck of the lamb (shoulder chops)

3 tbsp (50 mL) unsalted butter
4 medium potatoes, peeled and cut into 1/4-inch
    (5 mm) slices
2 tsp (10 mL) salt
1/2 tsp (2 mL) pepper
2 tbsp (25 mL) brown sugar
2 tsp (10 mL) chopped fresh parsley
4 lamb kidneys, fat and membranes removed, cut into
    1/4-inch (5 mm) slices (optional)
8 fresh or frozen oysters (not smoked)
2 cups (500 mL) sliced mushrooms
2 medium onions, chopped
2 cups (500 mL) beef stock

Trim the fat off the chops. Melt 2 tbsp (25 mL) of the butter in a saucepan over medium heat and brown the chops on both sides. Grease the bottom and sides of a deep 16-cup (4 L) casserole dish with the remaining butter.

Spread one-third of the potato slices in the dish and place 4 lamb chops side by side on top of them. Sprinkle the chops with half the salt, pepper, brown sugar, and parsley. Top with half the kidneys (if using), oysters, mushrooms, and onions. Cover with another third of the potatoes. Put the other 4 lamb chops on the potatoes and sprinkle them with the remaining salt, pepper, brown sugar, and parsley. Add the rest of the kidneys, oysters, mushrooms, and onions. Spread the remaining potatoes on top. Pour in the beef stock. Cover and bake at 350°F (180°C) for 1 1/2 hours. Remove the lid and bake for another 30 minutes or until the potatoes are browned. Serve directly from the casserole.

Note: This dish can be done in a crockpot, although it will not be possible to brown the potato slices. 🍂

Pork and Apple Pie

He was very late in returning—so late that I knew that the concert could not have detained him all the time. Dinner was on the table before he appeared.

A STUDY IN SCARLET

*I*t was in January of 1881 that Holmes and Watson first met and shortly thereafter moved into Baker Street together. *A Study in Scarlet* was the first investigation in which the good doctor participated. By this time it was March and he was beginning to get used to some of the strange ways of his fellow lodger. So was Mrs Hudson, who must have experienced considerable frustration in her attempts to schedule meals around a man who alternated periods of complete inertia with fits of working energy that saw him coming and going from his rooms at all hours.

This particular dish is something she could have prepared early in the evening and kept in the oven for his eventual reappearance. It is warm and filling, and particularly suited to London's late-winter weather. It can be made with a pastry crust, but potatoes are frequently used and make for a more substantial meal. It goes well with a green salad.

Serves 4–6

2 lb (1 kg) pork loin, fat and gristle removed,
cut into 1/2- inch (1 cm) pieces

1 tsp (5 mL) salt
4 medium cooking apples, peeled and cut into
    1/4-inch (5 mm) slices
1/4 cup (50 mL) brown sugar
1/4 cup (50 mL) white wine
1/4 cup (50 mL) beef stock
4 medium potatoes, peeled and quartered
3 tbsp (50 mL) butter
1/2 cup (125 mL) milk
Salt and pepper to taste

Place a third of the pork in a 12-cup (3 L) casserole dish. Sprinkle with half of the salt. Add a layer of half of the apples. Sprinkle on half of the sugar. Add another third of the pork, the remainder of the salt, and the rest of the apples and sugar. Place the remainder of the pork on top and pour in the wine and beef stock. Cover the dish tightly with foil and bake at 325°F (160°C) for 1 1/2 hours or until the pork is tender.

Meanwhile, boil the potatoes in enough lightly salted water to cover them until they are tender. Drain and mash with the butter and milk. Season with salt and pepper and keep warm.

Spread the potatoes evenly over the pork and bake, uncovered, in the upper third of the oven for 10 minutes or until the top is beginning to brown. Serve immediately. 🍎

Steak and Oyster Pie

"Now, look here, Mr Holmes, it's half-past eleven now and I am going back right away to my hotel. Suppose you and your friend Dr Watson, come round and lunch with us at two."

THE HOUND OF THE BASKERVILLES

*T*his lunch invitation was made by Sir Henry Baskerville, who had retained Holmes to investigate some mysterious threats of violence that had been made against his person. Sir Henry was staying at the Northumberland Hotel, which some Sherlockians feel might be another name for the Hotel Metropole in Northumberland Avenue, or the Grand Hotel in Trafalgar Square.

Watson records that he and Holmes had "a pleasant luncheon" with Sir Henry, although no mention is made of what they chose from the menu. However, both he and Holmes often showed a preference for beef, and given the Victorian affinity for beef with oysters, and oyster sauces, steak and oyster pie was a likely candidate.

Serves 4

1 1/2 lb (750 g) beef steak
2 tbsp (25 mL) unsalted butter
2 tbsp (25 mL) all-purpose flour
12 fresh or frozen oysters (not smoked)

2 tsp (10 mL) cornstarch (optional)
2 tsp (10 mL) oyster sauce
1/4 tsp (1 mL) salt
1/4 tsp (1 mL) pepper
Pastry for a 9-inch (23 cm) pie crust
1 egg yolk, beaten

Cut the meat into 1-inch (2.5 cm) cubes. Melt the butter in a saucepan over medium-high heat. Coat the steak pieces with the flour and fry them for a few minutes until they are brown on all sides. Put them in a shallow casserole dish, adding water just to cover. Cover and bake at 350°F (180°C) for 1 1/2 hours.

Pour the broth off the meat, reserving 1 cup (250 mL). Put the meat in a 9-inch (23 cm) pie dish and add the oysters. If the reserved broth is thin, mix the cornstarch with 2 tsp (10 mL) cold water and stir it in. Add the oyster sauce, salt, and pepper to the broth. Adjust seasoning, then stir the broth into the pie dish.

Roll out the pasty to cover the pie dish, crimp to seal the edges, and cut 2 or 3 slits to allow steam to escape. Brush all over with the egg yolk. Bake at 375°F (190°C) for 25 minutes or until pastry is golden. Serve hot. 🍎

Inky Pinky

"I must discuss it while I eat, for I have not much time. It is nearly five now. In two hours we must be on the scene of action."

A SCANDAL IN BOHEMIA

*I*t wasn't unusual for Holmes to eat a quick dinner in the midst of an investigation, in this instance one that involved the beautiful and talented Irene Adler, a woman who managed to defeat his attempts to recover a photograph that compromised his client, the King of Bohemia. In situations demanding a hurried meal Mrs Hudson could well have provided inky pinky, a traditional Scottish dish of leftover roast beef with carrots and gravy. Inky pinky is sometimes accompanied by slices of toast or mashed potatoes.

Serves 4–6

> 8 carrots
> 1 1/3 cups (325 mL) beef gravy
> 1 tsp (5 mL) vinegar
> Salt and pepper
> 1 tsp (5 mL) cornflour
> 8 slices cold roast beef, fat removed

Slice the carrots. Put them in a saucepan with water to cover and boil until just tender. Drain them and put them back in the saucepan along with the beef gravy. Heat until just simmering. Add the vinegar and season with salt and pepper to taste. Blend the cornflour with a little cold water, then add it to the gravy, stirring until the mixture thickens.

Add the roast beef, stirring for 2–3 minutes so that the slices are heated and coated with the gravy. Serve immediately. 🍎

Eggs and Cheese

The man whom I found myself facing was a well-built, fresh-complexioned young fellow, with a frank, honest face and a slight, crisp, yellow moustache. He wore a very shiny top-hat and a neat suit of sober black, which made him look what he was—a smart young City man, of the class who have been labelled cockneys ...

THE ADVENTURE OF THE STOCKBROKER'S CLERK

atson is referring here to Hall Pycroft, a young man who was duped into assisting the famous forger Beddington in a robbery of a London financial house. The doctor mentions that Pycroft is a Cockney, one of the many working-class Londoners of Holmes's acquaintance. There was a time when Cockney was a term of disdain used by country people to refer to soft city-dwellers, and it was also used by parents to describe a spoilt child before the term was taken up by bold and quirky East Londoners as a badge of pride. Its origin was in "cokeney" or "cock's egg," terms applied to the often misshapen eggs of domestic hens in the Middle Ages.

The medieval hen was expected to yield about 150 eggs a year, but their eggs were smaller than those of the present day, and their laying capacities were minimal during cold weather. However, the eggs of hens, ducks, geese, and even seabirds in coastal areas have long been part of the British diet. They could usually be eaten during religious fast days, except for Lent, and boiled eggs served with green sauce were traditional fare on

Easter Day. By the sixteenth century, recipes for "amulets" (omelets) were common, and eggs were also used in boiled sweet puddings, custard dishes, and pancake batters. They were added as bindings to sweet and savoury pies, and their yolks were mixed with spices and sugar, then gently heated with wine or ale and served as breakfast and bedtime drinks known as caudels. Their whites were useful as raising agents and later became the chief ingredient in the very popular French import, the meringue.

In 1847 Cochin China or "Shanghae" hens were introduced into Britain to an audience of astounded mid-Victorians. Even Queen Victoria was so taken with them that she added some Cochins to her poultry collection at Windsor. The secret of their success was their prolific laying capacity, even during the winter months. "In the morning I was up betimes, but some toast crumbs and two empty eggshells told me that my companion was earlier still," Dr Watson notes in *The Adventure of the Retired Colourman*. By that time the Cochin had played a significant part in a revolution that swept the traditional British morning repast of ale, bread and cheese off the table, and eggs, usually boiled, but often fried or scrambled, became an indispensable part of breakfast at 221b Baker Street and Victorian middle-class households throughout the land.

Cheese is another food with a long history in the British diet, and its roots are found in the simple, primitive activity of drawing off whey from the curds of sour milk, which were then squeezed into cakes and left to dry. The process later involved the addition of rennet, a digestive juice secreted in the stomachs of several mammals, to further ripen the curds and produce a hard cheese that could last through the winter.

Cheese was normally made by shepherds from the milk of ewes in lowland Britain during Anglo-Saxon times, although the inhabitants of Wales and northern England used cows' milk, and by the end of the medieval period cows were the dominant suppliers of milk for cheese. Cheese was classified according to texture: hard, made from skim milk; soft from whole milk; and "green" cheese, which was a fresh curd cheese that had to be eaten quickly. The skim-milk cheeses went to the peasants and the full-cream milk varieties went to the gentry. Later, cheese was classified by district, and by the seventeenth century there were noted cheese fairs in Wiltshire, Oxfordshire, Hampshire, and Warwickshire.

The soil of Cheshire contains sedimentary deposits that enrich the fodder of the local cattle, thereby enabling the production of a cheese that has always been popular. Quartermasters of British regiments in Scotland during the seventeenth-century civil war ordered three hundred tons of it for their troops. During Holmes's day, farmers used to pay their rents with it. Occasionally, Cheshire cheese develops a particular blue mould, and Pall Mall clubs such as Mycroft Holmes's Diogenes went to great lengths to make "Blue Cheshire" available to their members. Other cheeses already highly prized by the nineteenth century were the double Gloucesters from the Vale of Gloucester that were sent in fifty-pound rounds down the Thames in barges to London. Stilton had acquired its name as the finest of blue cheeses, and high value was also placed on the skimmed-milk Blue Viney of Dorset. Caerphilly, a soft white cheese, came into its own in Wales as an easily digestible miner's food, and Dunlop, a soft and creamy Scottish cheese, was very popular.

In 1840 the farmers of Somerset's Cheddar district produced, with the aid of 750 cows, a huge Cheddar cheese that weighed about 1,100 pounds and was ten feet in circumference. It was given to Queen Victoria as a wedding present and then put on exhibition. The Queen decided to return it to the farmers at the exhibition's close, but they argued over its ownership and the cheese, like some gigantic orphan, had to be taken into legal custody. Then it simply disappeared and was never heard of again. This was some years before Holmes began his investigative practice, otherwise Dr Watson might well have found himself scribbling notes in rural Somerset for *The Adventure of the Lost Cheddar*! ❦

Black Swan Cheese and Beer on Toast

The "Black Swan" is an inn of repute in the High Street ... and there we found the young lady waiting for us. She had engaged a sitting-room, and our lunch awaited us upon the table.

THE ADVENTURE OF THE COPPER BEECHES

The young lady waiting for Holmes and Watson was Miss Violet Hunter, a governess hired in mysterious circumstances by Mr Runcastle of Hampshire. Over their lunch Holmes deduced that these circumstances involved the imprisonment of Runcastle's step-daughter for purposes of acquiring her inheritance. Although we do not have a record of what was served, this beer and cheese dish might well have been on the menu.

Cheshire or double Gloucester is often specified for this recipe. If neither is available, a sharp Cheddar is a good substitute.

Serves 4

2 tbsp (25 mL) prepared mustard
3/4 cup (175 mL) strong beer
6 cups (1.5 L) shredded cheese (not packed down in the cup)
1 tsp (5 mL) salt
4 thick slices toast

In a saucepan whisk the mustard with half of the beer until thoroughly mixed. Heat over medium heat and gradually add cheese, whisking continuously. As cheese melts, add more beer until the mixture forms a thick sauce. Add the salt. Spoon over the toast and serve immediately.

Note: If the cheese and beer mixture is too strong in flavour, stir in 1 tsp (5 mL) of sugar. 🍎

Scotch Eggs

Holmes was sunk in profound thought, and hardly opened his mouth until we had passed Clapham Junction …

It was twenty past three when we reached our terminus, and after a hasty luncheon at the buffet we pushed on at once to Scotland Yard.

THE ADVENTURE OF THE NAVAL TREATY

The theft of an important British and Italian naval treaty from the office of Watson's old school chum Percy Phelps involves Holmes and the good doctor in a complex and active investigation. Their hasty luncheon at the station buffet might well have included Scotch eggs, something they were likely familiar with from Mrs Hudson's cooking. Scotch eggs can be eaten hot or served cold as a picnic food.

Serves 4–6

1/3 cup (75 mL) all-purpose flour
1 large egg, beaten
1 cup (250 mL) dry breadcrumbs
1 tsp (5 mL) salt
1/2 tsp (2 mL) pepper
1 lb (500 g) sausage meat
Oil for deep-frying
6 hard-boiled eggs

Have ready in three separate dishes the flour, beaten egg, and breadcrumbs. Mix the salt and pepper into the sausage meat. Divide the meat into six portions. In a deep-fryer, heat oil to 400°F (200°C).

Dust the hard-boiled eggs with flour, then with floured hands mould one portion of sausage meat around each egg, covering it completely. Dip the eggs into the beaten egg, letting the excess drip off, then roll in the breadcrumbs. Deep-fry the eggs until brown (5–6 minutes). Alternatively, bake eggs on a lightly oiled baking sheet at 350°F (180°C) until the meat is thoroughly cooked (about 30 minutes). Serve hot or cold.

Note: Many supermarkets sell packages of sausage meat or ground pork. If these are not available, purchase pork sausages and remove the casings. 🍎

Scotch Woodcock

"I have one or two things which I would wish to do now that I am in town. But I shall return by the twelve o'clock train, so as to be there in time for your coming."

"And you may expect us early in the afternoon. I have myself some small business matters to attend to. Will you not wait and break-fast?"

"No, I must go. My heart is lightened already since I have confided my trouble to you." She dropped her thick black veil over her face, and glided from the room.

THE ADVENTURE OF THE SPECKLED BAND

*H*olmes undertook several investigations involving unpleasant men who attempted to do away with their step-daughters over their inheritance, but Dr Grimsby Roylott of Stoke Moran, who attempted to murder Miss Julie Stoner with a poisonous swamp adder from India, was probably the nastiest.

Miss Stoner left with a lightened heart after her initial consultation at Baker Street, but Roylott himself, who is described by Watson as resembling a "furious bird of prey," marched into their lodgings and threatened Holmes. It was only after his departure that they were able to sit down to breakfast.

This recipe, adapted from Dr W. Kitchiner's *The Cook's Oracle* (1840), makes for a distinctive breakfast dish that would have intrigued Holmes.

Serves 2–4

> 4 anchovies
> 4 egg yolks
> 1/3 cup (75 mL) table (18%) cream
> 4 slices hot buttered toast

Reduce the anchovies to a paste with a fork. Beat the egg yolks well in a heatproof bowl or top of a double boiler, then stir in the cream. Heat the egg mixture over boiling water, stirring continuously, until it thickens enough to coat the back of a wooden spoon. Do not allow it to boil. Spread one-quarter of the anchovy paste on each piece of toast. Pour eggs over toast and serve immediately.

Note: About 1 tsp (5 mL) prepared anchovy paste or essence may be used in place of anchovies.

This is definitely not a recipe for those who have no fondness for anchovies. 🐝

Fried Ox Eyes

"I am sure, Mr Holmes, that we are very much indebted to you for having cleared the matter up. I wish I knew how you reach your results."

"I reached this one," said my friend, "by sitting upon five pillows and consuming an ounce of shag. I think, Watson, that if we drive to Baker Street we shall just be in time for breakfast."

THE MAN WITH THE TWISTED LIP

The matter that Holmes cleared up involved the disappearance of Mr Neville St Clair, a respectable man of the City, who secretly transformed his appearance every day into one of poverty and rags and made a successful living as a beggar. The case was an unusual and difficult one, and by the time Holmes had solved it early one morning he was probably very much looking forward to his breakfast.

This interesting fried egg recipe, adapted from Mrs Beeton's *Book of Household Management* (1861), would have appealed to both Holmes and Watson.

Serves 4

4 slices bread
2 tbsp (25 mL) butter
1/4 cup (50 mL) sour cream
1/4 cup (50 mL) chopped fresh parsley
4 eggs
Salt and pepper

With a knife or a large cookie cutter, cut each slice of bread into a large circle. Cut a 1 1/2-inch (4 cm) hole in the centre of each and toast the slices.

Melt the butter in a large frying pan over medium-low heat; lay in the toast and place 1 tbsp (15 mL) of sour cream in each hole. Sprinkle with parsley. Break an egg on top of the sour cream; sprinkle with salt and pepper to taste. Fry, without flipping, to desired consistency. If the egg is to be cooked hard, fry on a lower heat and cover the pan. Serve at once.

Note: Well-drained yogurt (drain it in a coffee filter overnight) may be substituted for the sour cream, and the butter may be eliminated by using a nonstick frying pan. 🍒

Savoury Eggs

"I must really apologize, Hopkins," said Sherlock Holmes; "I fear that the scrambled eggs are cold. However, you will enjoy the rest of your breakfast all the better, will you not, for the thought that you have brought your case to a triumphant conclusion?"

Stanley Hopkins was speechless with amazement.

THE ADVENTURE OF BLACK PETER

*I*t was Holmes's successful identification of the whale harpooner Patrick Cairns as the murderer of "Black Peter" Carey that left the young police officer Stanley Hopkins speechless. It does not appear from Watson's account that Hopkins ever managed to eat the breakfast Mrs Hudson cooked that morning, although both he and Holmes probably finished theirs. This Victorian recipe for savoury eggs is something they would have enjoyed.

Serves 2–4

> 1 tbsp (15 mL) butter or oil
> 1 small onion, finely chopped
> 1/2 cup (125 mL) chopped ham
> 1 tbsp (15 mL) chopped fresh parsley
> Pinch pepper
> 4 eggs
> 2 tbsp (25 mL) milk or cream
> 1/4 tsp (1 mL) salt

Melt the butter in a saucepan over medium heat and cook the onion, stirring occasionally, until it is transparent. Stir in the ham, parsley, and pepper. Spread the mixture in an oiled shallow casserole dish. Beat the eggs with the milk and salt. Pour the eggs over the ham mixture and bake at 350°F (180°C) until the eggs are set (about 20 minutes). Serve at once. 🐦

Food of the Chase

"My dear Watson," said a voice, "you have not even condescended to say good morning."

I turned in incontrollable astonishment. The aged ecclesiastic had turned his face towards me. For an instant the wrinkles were smoothed away, the nose drew away from the chin, the lower lip ceased to protrude and the mouth to mumble, the dull eyes regained their fire, the drooping figure expanded. The next the whole frame collapsed, and Holmes had gone as quickly as he had come.

"Good heavens!" I cried. "How you startled me!"

"Every precaution is still necessary," he whispered. "I have reason to think that they are hot upon our trail. Ah, there is Moriarity himself."

THE ADVENTURE OF THE FINAL PROBLEM

olmes was a true magician of disguise. In this case he made himself up as an elderly Italian priest in order to deceive Professor Moriarity, the arch criminal who was determined to murder him. For three years after he supposedly plunged to his death at Reichenbach Fall while locked in a deadly embrace with the same sinister fiend, Holmes cloaked himself in a variety of personae—as an explorer in Tibet, where he met the Dalai Lama; as a pilgrim in Mecca and Khartoum; and as a French chemist in a laboratory in Montpelier, before finally returning to England and entering Watson's study disguised as an old book collector, an encounter that not only occasioned astonishment but caused his old friend to faint "for the first and the last time in my life."

"Our quest does not appear to take us to very fashionable regions," he said quite casually to Watson at one point, and his shape-changing abilities must have been particularly valuable in cases that took him into the more dangerous and murky areas of London's underworld. In *The Man with the Twisted Lip* adventure he managed to go unnoticed as an old addict in a highly disreputable opium den east of London Bridge. He was also familiar with a number of the urchin and orphan boys from the destitute areas of the city, employing up to a dozen of them at times as spies and invaluable street informants. Normally the boys lived off scraps of food thrown into the alleys, but he paid them well and it must have been a joy for them to be able to choose from among the rich variety of foods hawked on the streets by costermongers. There were many occasions on which Holmes, in order to maintain the veracity of his disguise, would have become quite familiar with some of these items. After all, he could hardly have sauntered into Simpson's or the Café Royal in the bewhiskered sailor in an ancient pea jacket incarnation he assumed in *The Sign of Four*.

Nevertheless, he would have eaten well. If he was inclined to seafood there were plenty of stalls and shops selling hot eels, eel pies, pickled shellfish such as whelks, oysters, and fried fish and chips, the latter being a meal rapidly growing in popularity among the working class. He may have had second thoughts about some of the beverages on offer, aware perhaps from his own researches that ginger-beer, for example—of which an estimated 300,000 gallons were sold per annum in London in those days—was often boiled up in the same copper vessels used by lodgers for washing their dirty linen. He may also have had his reservations about some of the other drinks, such as lemonade, peppermint water, and Persian sherbet. Severe outbreaks of cholera in Victorian England sparked an awareness of a hitherto unsuspected link between impure water and disease. This and the fact that the Thames was so contaminated with foul-smelling sewage that the houses of Parliament were sometimes unable to sit during hot weather may have led him to conclude that he was better off with some of the boiled drinks, such as tea or coffee, or beer bottled with safe water.

Was he tempted by sheep trotters? Perhaps not. Holmes seems to have been a beef man, and when he informs Watson in *The Adventure of the Crooked Man* that "I had some supper at Waterloo," he is likely referring to boiled meat puddings or steak and kidney pies. A quick meal snatched in a local inn likely included pickled eggs or onions, and a ham sandwich along with a pint of bitter. A dinner in one of the poorer East End neighbourhoods might have featured a plate of the famous left-over potato, cabbage, and beef fry-up known as bubble and squeak.

There was also a considerable street trade in apples and oranges, although strawberries, bought by the costermongers at Covent Garden and retailed in their barrows during the early summer weeks, were the particular favourite. Fruits such as rhubarb, gooseberries, cherries, apples, cranberries, and damsons were cooked in tarts, and Holmes would have had his pick of mince pies, gingerbread, muffins, crumpets, plum duff, and many other types of buns and cakes.

Of course there were times when Holmes brought food with him on his expeditions, usually in the form of sandwiches he purchased at local inns or brought with him from Baker Street. It is not hard to imagine Mrs Hudson puzzling over her famous lodger's remarkable talents for disguise when this occurred. It has been said that he may have toured America as an actor with the Sasanoff Shakespearean Company between 1879 and 1880, or was trained by out-of-work or retired actors in London. In any case, his appearance must have unnerved her at times, and his masquerade as a Nonconformist clergyman in the *Scandal in Bohemia* affair probably caused her to miss a step or two in the "stately tread" of her bearing that Watson refers to at one point. Perhaps on these occasions she was tempted to insist that the greatest detective of his day make his own sandwiches. 🍏

Bohemian Scandal
Pickled Eggs

"I lent the ostlers a hand in rubbing down their horses, and I received in exchange twopence, a glass of half-and-half, two fills of shag tobacco, and as much information as I could desire about Miss Adler ..."

A SCANDAL IN BOHEMIA

*H*olmes, in disguise as a groom (a servant who looks after horses), discovered a great deal about Irene Adler, a fascinating woman who refused to part with a photograph that compromised the King of Bohemia. Holmes often drank beer during his undercover work as a labourer, and in such situations he also likely ate his share of pickled eggs, as they were a common accompaniment to beer.

Eggs were traditionally pickled around Easter when farm chickens were at their best laying period. Pickled eggs go well with cold meat and cheese. Beer is a must.

Makes 12 pickled eggs

> 12 eggs
> 4 cups (1 L) malt vinegar

Boil the eggs for 10 minutes. Run them under cold water until they are cool enough to handle and remove the shells. Put the eggs in a 10-cup (2.5 L) wide-mouth jar with a tight-fitting lid. Bring the malt vinegar to a boil in a saucepan. Let it cool for 1 minute, then pour it over the eggs, leaving a 1/2-inch (1 cm) space at the top of the jar. Seal the jar. Store in a cool, dark place. The eggs will be ready in 2–3 weeks. They should be brown on the outside and their yolks should be soft and creamy. ❦

Fried Fish and Chips

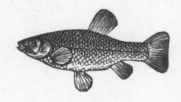

I saw in the papers that he had been engaged by the French government upon a matter of supreme importance, and I received two notes from Holmes, dated from Narbonne and from Nîmes, from which I gathered that his stay in France was likely to be a long one.

THE ADVENTURE OF THE FINAL PROBLEM

Holmes's fluent French enabled him to work easily at all levels of French society. Perhaps it was during the period Watson is referring to that he became acquainted with "chipped" potatoes. Fried-fish shops had been around in England since the 1850s, but once chipped potatoes were introduced from France in the 1870s fish and chips quickly became a mainstay in the working-class diet in London and the northern industrial towns.

One of the secrets of successful fish and chips is to use fish that is fresh. The quality of frozen fish is always questionable and its moisture content can be hard to gauge after it has been defrosted; this can make for difficulties with the batter.

Serves 4

BATTER
1 cup (250 mL) all-purpose flour
1 tsp (5 mL) baking powder

1 egg yolk
1/4 tsp (1 mL) salt
1/4 cup (50 mL) beer
3 tbsp (50 mL) milk
3 tbsp (50 mL) water
2 egg whites

CHIPS

4 medium potatoes, peeled and cut into 1/4 –1/2-inch
    (5 mm –1 cm) chips
2 lb (1 kg) fresh skinned fillets of white-fleshed fish such as
    cod or sole, cut into 3 x 5 inches (8 x 12 cm) pieces
2 tbsp (25 mL) all-purpose flour seasoned with salt and pepper
Oil for frying

Sift the flour with the baking powder. In a large bowl beat together the egg yolk, salt, beer, milk, and water. Beat in the flour until the batter is smooth and adheres to the back of a wooden spoon. Let stand for 30 minutes. Beat the egg whites until they form soft peaks and gently fold them into the batter.

Heat 4–5 inches (10–12 cm) of oil to 375°F (190°C) in a deep-fryer. If the potato chips have been immersed in water, dry them well on paper towels. Deep-fry them in 1 1/2-cup (375 mL) batches until golden brown. Drain, then transfer each batch to a baking sheet in a warm oven.

Wash the fish in cold water and dry completely. Dust lightly with the seasoned flour, then dip each piece in the batter. Fry them in the deep-fryer for 5 minutes or until golden brown. Serve immediately with the chips, malt vinegar, and salt. ❦

Pickled Onions

"The question now is whether we should take a premature lunch here, or run our chance of starving before we reach the buffet at Newhaven."

THE ADVENTURE OF THE FINAL PROBLEM

*H*olmes is speaking as he and Watson have alighted from a train at Canterbury to evade the clutches of the master criminal, Professor Moriarity. It is noteworthy that even in times of intense danger Holmes could think of food, and given the reputation of some railway eatables, he likely chose to go to a local inn, where they could have a quick but tasty meal, perhaps along the lines of the traditional "ploughman's lunch" fare of thick chunks of bread and cheese with a piquant condiment, such as pickled onions.

Pickled onions go well with most types of simple foods including fish and chips, cold beef, or ham. The onions prepared in this recipe will keep their crispness and flavour for up to six months after bottling.

Makes about 5 cups (1.25 L)

2 lb (1 kg) white (pearl) onions, about 1 inch (2.5 cm)
in diameter
1/2 cup (125 mL) coarse salt

5 cups (1.25 L) malt vinegar
1/2 cup (125 mL) sugar
2 tbsp (25 mL) pickling spice
1 inch (2.5 cm) fresh ginger, chopped
10 black peppercorns
5 whole cloves

Put the onions in a bowl and cover with boiling water; let stand for 5 minutes. Drain and plunge them into ice water. Drain again and carefully remove their skins with a sharp knife. Return them to the bowl, sprinkle them with the salt, and turn each onion to be sure it is coated. Cover the bowl and let it stand in a cool place overnight. Drain and rinse the onions several times under cold running water.

In a large saucepan bring the vinegar, sugar, pickling spice, ginger, peppercorns, and cloves to a boil, stirring until the sugar dissolves. Boil for 5 minutes, then add the onions. Bring to a boil again, and boil for 10 minutes.

Remove the onions with a slotted spoon and put them into sterilized jars. Strain the vinegar mixture to remove the spices and pour it over the onions, filling the jars to within 1/2 inch (1 cm) of the top. Store in a cool, dark place. 🍒

Priory School Parkin

The day was just breaking when I woke to find the long, thin form of Holmes by my bedside. He was fully dressed, and had apparently already been out.

"I have done the lawn and the bicycle shed," said he. "I have also had a ramble through the Ragged Shaw. Now, Watson, there is cocoa ready in the next room. I must beg you to hurry, for we have a great day before us."

THE ADVENTURE OF THE PRIORY SCHOOL

Holmes and Watson were in the north of England, on the second day of a search for the young Lord Saltire, who, from all appearances, had been abducted from his select preparatory school, The Priory. Perhaps the good doctor, in addition to snatching a quick cup of cocoa, managed to pocket some parkin. Parkin is a traditional type of rich gingerbread made with oatmeal. It is common in Scotland and northern England, and is usually baked as a cake, though it also appears as biscuits. Dr Watson had a sweet tooth and would have found it a nourishing comfort after having been rushed out of bed by Holmes.

Serves 6

1 cup (250 mL) brown sugar
3/4 cup (175 mL) unsalted butter
1/2 cup (125 mL) molasses
1 1/2 cups (375 mL) cake-and-pastry flour
2 tsp (10 mL) baking soda
2 tsp (10 mL) ginger
2 tsp (10 mL) cinnamon
1/4 tsp (1 mL) salt
1 1/4 cups (300 mL) quick-cooking oatmeal
2 large eggs, beaten
1 cup (250 mL) hot water

Melt the sugar, butter, and molasses together in a small saucepan over low heat. Set aside to cool.

Sift the flour, baking soda, ginger, cinnamon, and salt into a bowl, then mix in the oatmeal. Stir in the molasses mixture and beaten eggs, then stir in the hot water. Pour the batter into a greased 13- x 9-inch (3.5 L) cake pan. Bake at 350°F (180°C) for 45 minutes or until the cake is springy to the touch.

Cool on a rack and serve with tea, coffee, or hot chocolate. 🦃

Railway Journey Egg Sandwiches

"We have, I think, just time to catch our train at Paddington, and I will go further into the matter upon our journey. You could oblige me by bringing with you your very excellent field glass."

And so it happened that an hour or so later I found myself in the corner of a first-class carriage, flying along, en route for Exeter, while Sherlock Holmes, with his sharp, eager face framed in his ear-flapped travelling-cap, dipped rapidly into the bundle of fresh papers which he had procured at Paddington.

THE ADVENTURE OF SILVER BLAZE

*I*n the Silver Blaze affair, Holmes and Watson set out from Paddington to investigate the disappearance of a famous race horse. In addition to field glasses, travelling-caps, and newspapers they likely brought with them sandwiches for the journey to Exeter, a trip that took them all day.

A Victorian sandwich for a long trip was often made with a thick slice of toast. This was slit open and the filling was inserted in the toast much as with a pita bread. This prevented sogginess on the journey.

Makes 4 sandwiches

DRESSING

1 egg yolk

3 tbsp (50 mL) table (18%) cream

2 tbsp (25 mL) finely chopped fresh parsley

2 tbsp (25 mL) salad oil

1 tbsp (15 mL) white wine vinegar

2 tsp (10 mL) sugar

1/2 tsp (2 mL) salt

1/2 tsp (2 mL) white pepper

1/4 tsp (1 mL) dry mustard

4 hard-boiled eggs, finely chopped

4 thick slices toast, cooled

Blend the dressing ingredients together until smooth and set aside.

Put the chopped eggs in a bowl and mix in the dressing to taste, bearing in mind that the sandwich filling should not be overly moist.

Make pockets for the filling with a sharp knife in one side of each piece of toast, making sure not to puncture the other sides. Put a portion of the filling in each piece of toast. Wrap in foil or plastic wrap so that the filling stays in. Store in a cool place until ready to eat. 🐛

Bubble and Squeak

"I want you, Mr Hall Pycroft, to tell my friend your very interesting experience exactly as you have told it to me, or with more detail if possible."

THE ADVENTURE OF THE STOCKBROKER'S CLERK

*H*all Pycroft was a Cockney who was tricked into assisting with an attempted robbery. Holmes would have been familiar with bubble and squeak, a famous Cockney dish consisting of fried-up leftover meat and vegetables. One of several derivations of its name can be found in Cockney rhyming slang for "the end of the week"—when all that remained in the larder was tossed into a frying pan and heated up.

Serves 3–4

    3 tbsp (50 mL) butter
    2 tbsp (25 mL) all-purpose flour
    1 cup (250 mL) beef stock
    2 tbsp (25 mL) tomato ketchup
    2 1/2 cups (625 mL) mashed or diced boiled potatoes
    2 cups (500 mL) cooked chopped cabbage or other
        green vegetable, such as brussels sprouts
    2 cups (500 mL) cooked meat cut into bite-sized pieces
    Salt and pepper

Melt half of the butter in a saucepan over medium heat, then add the flour and cook for 1 minute, stirring constantly. Whisk in the beef stock and stir until thickened. Stir in the ketchup. Keep the gravy warm.

Melt the remaining butter in a frying pan over medium-high heat and stir in the potatoes, cabbage, and meat. Fry the mixture, turning occasionally as it browns and is heated through. Stir in the gravy and salt and pepper to taste. Serve immediately. 🍎

Breads and Cakes

t was in 1760, more than a century before Holmes made his sandwich suggestion to Watson, that John Montague, the fourth Earl of Sandwich, invented his culinary namesake. Montague saw the sandwich as something that he could eat while continuing to gamble, a pastime that preoccupied him far more than his dining hour. The earl's sandwich was, of course, dependent on a supply of bread in his cook's larder, which was in turn dependent on grain and a means of milling it into flour.

While Holmes was still a young undergraduate at university, a revolution in flour milling took place that was to have considerable social consequences. In 1872 the first mill to use porcelain rollers was introduced in Britain in Glasgow, and six years later a roller mill in Liverpool was producing three thousand sacks of flour a week. By 1890 the age-old process of stone grinding grain had been largely supplanted by roller-mill operations. They were quicker, less costly to maintain, and milled a flour with a much longer storage life. They also made it possible to sift off the germ of the wheat with the bran, thereby producing a much whiter flour, a commodity held in high social regard for centuries.

It appears that the initial discriminatory notions with regard to flour were introduced into Britain by the Romans. They required large quantities of grain to sustain their armies of occupation after their first successful invasion of the country in AD 43, and brought with them soft wheats that enabled fine white flours to be sifted off from the darker and coarser hulls. "To know the colour of one's bread" was the Roman expression for knowing one's place in a society where the wealthy ate bread of fine white flour and the poorer civilians and soldiers ate rougher dark bread often made from barley and other grains.

During the Anglo-Saxon period wheaten bread was considered "clean" when made from finely sifted flour, and "common" when more coarsely sieved. The colour white was also held in particular esteem during the Middle Ages, and "wastel" (from the Norman French *gastel*, or cake) was their best grade of white wheaten flour. Later, the term "manchet" was applied to white flour. However, the presence of wheat germ in both manchet and wastel would have given them a creamy yellowish colour not found in roller-milled flours. In the thirteenth century professional bakers were divided into white and brown guilds, and a loaf of medieval brown bread that sold for a farthing was supposed to weigh twice as much as a loaf of white bread of the same price.

Whiter grades of flour were also required in cakes, although there was a fine line between breads and cakes at that time. A fourteenth-century recipe from Salisbury called "Wastels y Farced" is for an enriched bread made with eggs, butter, sugar, spices, and currants. The name "short-paste" was given to both bread and cakes; further confusion arose when "cake" was used to refer to a piece of bread. In Scotland, the ambivalence has been maintained in one of the more famous contributions to bakery—shortbread. Gingerbread, another well-known bread-cake crossover, was made in the Middle Ages with compacted breadcrumbs, honey, and spices, and coloured red with the addition of sandalwood. Small sweet cakes of short-paste flavoured with spices were popular at banquets during the Elizabethan era and were often boxed along with other cake breads and biscuits and kept until needed. Large cakes, which retained the character of medieval enriched breads, were raised with yeast and baked in bread ovens, while small cakes were baked after the bread loaves had been finished and the ovens began to cool.

The popularity of white flour continued to grow during the seventeenth century, particularly among urban artisans, who felt that it more suited their sensitive digestions than it did those of country labourers. It continued to be demanded for cakes, which became much lighter in weight as cheaper sugar from abroad replaced some of the dried fruit that had provided sweetness in their medieval counterparts. Another change was the replacement of yeast or ale leaven with eggs as a cake-raising agent. As agricultural methods improved in the 1800s and wheat became more available, white bread gained favour among all classes, and some unscrupulous bakers began to use adulterants such as alum, chalk, lime, white lead, and ground bones from charnel houses to lighten the colour of their flour. It wasn't until 1872 that the use of such substances was proscribed by law.

Once Britain's wheat was milled by the new porcelain rollers, the historic class battle over white flour ended with white bread available to rich and poor alike. It has been pointed out that this was no great victory for the latter. The production of the new flour entailed the loss of the germ of the wheat and with it a large percentage of the flour's vitamin B1, nicotinic acid, and iron. The labouring class had always depended on large amounts of bread in their diet, and the waxen, sickly look common to the faces Holmes and Watson saw when their investigations took them into the poorer sections of Victorian London can be to a large degree attributed to roller-milled flour. However, other grains continued to be used in bread making, particularly outside the urban centres. Barley bread was still made in Cornwall, Wales, and Scotland, rye bread was eaten in Norfolk and Suffolk, and very coarse breads that included pea and bean meal in their flours were still being baked in some areas. We can also be assured that Holmes and Watson benefited, nutrient-wise, from the sensible approach of Mrs Hudson, who would have included oatmeal in her baking, two examples of which can be found in the oatmeal scones and oatcake recipes provided in this chapter. 🍎

Five Orange Pips Flapjack

It was in the latter days of September, and the equinoctial gales had set in with exceptional violence ... Sherlock Holmes sat moodily at one side of the fireplace cross-indexing his records of crime, while I at the other was deep in one of Clark Russell's fine sea-stories, until the howl of the gale from without seemed to blend with the text, and the splash of the rain to lengthen out into the long swash of the sea waves.

THE FIVE ORANGE PIPS

This recipe produces a very rich, and virtually irresistible, oatmeal snack food. Oats are a primary source of Scottish hardiness and energy, and Mrs Hudson may well have tempted Holmes and Watson with pieces of flapjack and tea on chilly autumn evenings.

Serves 4–6

> 1/2 cup (125 mL) unsalted butter
> 1 cup (250 mL) brown sugar
> 3 tbsp (50 mL) golden syrup
> 1 tbsp (15 mL) molasses
> 2 1/2 cups (625 mL) quick-cooking oatmeal
> 1 1/2 tsp (7 mL) cinnamon
> 2 tbsp (25 mL) whisky

Melt the butter in a saucepan over medium heat. Add the sugar, syrup, and molasses; stir until the sugar is dissolved. Stir in the oatmeal and cinnamon until combined thoroughly. Pour batter into a well-greased 8-inch (2 L) square cake pan. Bake at 350°F (180°C) until the edges begin to crisp (12–15 minutes). Sprinkle on the whisky. Let the flapjack remain in the pan until just warm to the touch, then cut it into squares.

Serve accompanied with tea, coffee, or hot chocolate. 🐾

Copper Beeches Crumpets

It was a cold morning of the early spring, and we sat after breakfast on either side of a cheery fire in the old room in Baker Street. A thick fog rolled down between the lines of dun-coloured houses, and the opposing windows loomed like dark, shapeless blurs, through the heavy yellow wreaths. Our gas was lit, and shone on the white cloth, and glimmer of china and metal, for the table had not been cleared yet.

THE ADVENTURE OF THE COPPER BEECHES

*H*olmes and Watson were about to begin an investigation that was to take them deep into rural Hampshire, and from Watson's description it does sound like an ideal morning for crumpets, perhaps even toasted over the fire.

Makes about 12 crumpets

> 2 tbsp (25 mL) lukewarm water
> 1 package dry yeast (1 tbsp/15 mL)
> 1/2 tsp (2 mL) sugar
> 1 cup (250 mL) cake-and-pastry flour
> 1/2 tsp (2 mL) salt
> 1 egg
> 3/4 cup (175 mL) milk at room temperature
> 1 tbsp (15 mL) unsalted butter, softened

Grease six 3-inch (8 cm) flan rings or 3-inch (8 cm) small tins such as tuna or salmon tins with the tops and bottoms removed.

Put the lukewarm water into a bowl. Stir in the yeast and sugar. Leave the bowl in a warm place for 5 minutes.

Meanwhile, sift the flour with the salt into a large bowl. Make a well in the centre and add the yeast, egg, milk, and butter. Beat until the batter is smooth. Drape a towel over the bowl and set aside in a warm place for 1 hour or until the batter has doubled in volume.

Grease a heavy frying pan large enough to hold the flan rings. Heat the frying pan over medium heat and lay the rings in it. Drop about 2 tbsp (25 mL) of batter into each ring. When the crumpets bubble, remove the rings and turn the crumpets over. Cook them for another 1–2 minutes or until they are firm and just beginning to brown on the bottom. Transfer to a baking sheet and keep warm. Grease the rings and repeat with remaining batter.

Serve for breakfast with butter, jam, or syrup. If the crumpets have been allowed to cool, reheat them in a toaster. 🍎

Boscombe Valley
Blackberry Roll

It was nearly four o'clock when we at last, after passing through the beautiful Stroud Valley, and over the broad gleaming Severn, found ourselves at the pretty little country town of Ross.

THE BOSCOMBE VALLEY MYSTERY

The Boscombe Valley affair took place during warm summer days in rural Hampshire in perfect weather for berry picking. This is an old recipe, which makes use of the abundant blackberries in rural hedgerows. Perhaps Holmes and Watson enjoyed Blackberry Roll at the Hereford Arms, where they stayed during their investigation.

Serves 4–6

2 cups (500 mL) cake-and-pastry flour
2 tsp (10 mL) baking powder
1 tsp (5 mL) baking soda
1/2 tsp (2 mL) salt
1/2 cup (125 mL) unsalted butter, softened
1/2 cup (125 mL) (approx.) milk
2 cups (500 mL) blackberries
1/4 cup (50 mL) brown sugar

1 tsp (5 mL) cinnamon
1/4 tsp (1 mL) ginger
1 tbsp (15 mL) unsalted butter, melted

Sift flour, baking powder, baking soda, and salt together into a large bowl. Rub in softened butter. Stir in enough of the milk to make a soft dough. Knead dough into a ball. On a lightly floured surface, roll out dough to a 1/2-inch (1 cm) thick rectangle approximately 12 x 8 inches (30 x 20 cm).

Cover evenly with berries, sugar, cinnamon, and ginger. Roll up from the long end into a "Swiss roll" shape. Crimp the ends together to seal and place on a greased baking sheet with the seam down. Brush with the melted butter and bake at 400°F (200°C) until golden brown (25–30 minutes). Slice and serve warm.

Note: Other berries, such as blueberries, may be substituted.❦

Oxford Cider Cake

It was in the year '95 that a combination of events, into which I need not enter, caused Mr Sherlock Holmes and myself to spend some weeks in one of our great University towns, and it was during this time that the small but instructive adventure which I am about to relate befell us.

THE ADVENTURE OF THE THREE STUDENTS

𝒜 serious theft of examination papers involving students of St. Luke's College had taken place and Holmes was called upon to investigate and avert a serious scandal. The university is clearly Oxford, and perhaps when he and Watson had solved the case they were rewarded with cider cake, an old favourite in Oxfordshire and several of the cider-producing West Counties. This cake is a variation of a nineteenth-century recipe and goes very well with lightly sweetened whipped cream.

Serves 4–6

> 1/2 cup (125 mL) unsalted butter
> 1 cup (250 mL) dark brown sugar
> 3 eggs, well beaten
> 2 cups (500 mL) cake-and-pastry flour
> 1 tsp (5 mL) cinnamon

1 tsp (5 mL) baking powder
1/2 tsp (2 mL) baking soda
1/4 tsp (1 mL) nutmeg
1/3 cup (75 mL) chopped walnuts
1 cup (250 mL) cider

In a large bowl, cream the butter and sugar. Mix in the eggs. Sift the flour with the cinnamon, baking powder, baking soda, and nutmeg. Add half the flour to the creamed mixture and beat well with a whisk or electric mixer. Stir in the walnuts, then the cider. Add the remaining flour and beat again. Pour into a greased 9-inch (2.5 L) square cake pan and bake at 375°F (190°C) for 40 minutes, or until an inserted toothpick comes out clean.

Let cool before turning out of pan. 🦌

Oatmeal
Cream Girdle Scones

Sharp at the hour named Inspector Stanley Hopkins appeared, and we sat down together to the excellent breakfast which Mrs Hudson had prepared. The young detective was in high spirits at his success.

THE ADVENTURE OF BLACK PETER

*I*n the Black Peter case, Stanley Hopkins, a young police inspector and great admirer of Holmes's scientific methods of deduction, arrived for a breakfast at Baker Street that was highlighted by the capture of a murderer. One feature of the excellent breakfast Mrs Hudson prepared for this unusual event might have been her oatmeal scones. They are very good at any time of the day, particularly when served warm with butter and jam. These scones are cooked in a heavy frying pan and are quite light in consistency.

Makes 8 scones

> 1 1/2 cups (375 mL) cake-and-pastry flour
> 1 tbsp (15 mL) baking powder
> 1/3 cup (75 mL) quick-cooking oatmeal
> 1/4 cup (50 mL) butter, cut into small pieces

2 eggs, well beaten
1/2 cup (125 mL) table (18%) cream

Sift the flour and baking powder together into a bowl; stir in the oatmeal. Rub in butter and beat in the eggs. Make a well in the centre and pour in the cream. Stir to create a soft, elastic dough. On a floured surface, roll the dough out to a 3/4-inch (2 cm) thickness. Divide the dough in half. Divide each half into four and form into rough biscuit shapes.

Place the scones in a moderately hot, lightly oiled heavy frying pan. Cook for 10–12 minutes, turning once as they brown. Serve warm with butter and jam. 🍎

Norway Expedition Oatcakes

"If you want me for the trial, my address and that of Watson will be somewhere in Norway—I'll send particulars later."

THE ADVENTURE OF BLACK PETER

Mrs Hudson, with her native Scottish foresight, would have wanted Holmes and Watson to carry something light and nourishing on their longer expeditions. The odds are that a good supply of oatcakes went along with them.

Makes about 16 oatcakes

> 3 cups (750 mL) quick-cooking oatmeal
> 1/2 tsp (2 mL) salt
> 1/4 tsp (1 mL) baking soda
> 3 tbsp (50 mL) unsalted butter, melted
> 1/2 cup (125 mL) (approx.) hot water

In a bowl stir together the oatmeal, salt, and baking soda. Pour in the melted butter, then stir in enough water to make a stiff dough. Turn the dough onto a floured surface and, working quickly with well-floured hands, knead it for 30 seconds. Roll the dough out to 1/4-inch (5 mm) thickness and cut out cakes with 3-inch (8 cm) cookie cutter or glass jar. Transfer to a lightly greased baking sheet and bake at 325°F (160°C) for 30 minutes or until the oatcakes just begin to brown. Cool on a rack.

Store the oatcakes buried in oatmeal in a meal chest or airtight tin. Some people prefer to reheat them before serving, but this is not necessary. They go very well with butter and honey or jam. 🦋

Desserts

Holmes pulled a large sheet of tissue-paper out of his pocket and carefully unfolded it upon his knee.

"What do you make of that?" he asked.

The paper was covered with the tracings of the footmarks of some small animal. It had five well-marked footpads, an indication of long nails, and the whole print might be nearly as large as a dessert-spoon.

THE ADVENTURE OF THE CROOKED MAN

he footmarks on the tissue paper were those of a pet mongoose belonging to Corporal Henry Wood, formerly of the 117th Foot Battalion in India. It is interesting that Watson compares the length of the prints to that of a spoon he refers to as a "dessert-spoon." "Dessert" was the proper Victorian middle- and upper-class nomenclature for the sweet dish that generally followed the main courses of a meal. Henry Wood, who describes himself as a "harum-scarum, reckless lad" with little education, would have called a dessert a pudding, a term with a long history in British culinary tradition that also quite accurately described the most popular type of dessert dish of Holmes's day.

The great Scottish poet Robert Burns once described the haggis as the "Great Chieftain o' the puddin' race!" indicating that the pudding was a dish with savoury, and not sweet, origins. However, the haggis, with its combination of entrails boiled in the stomach of a sheep, is actually more of a sausage than a pudding, although both were products of medieval autumn hog-killing. The pudding, known then as "black" pudding, was made of pig blood, diced fat, spices, and minced onions stuffed into lengths of intestine, and was boiled in water before being eaten. In those days there were also puddings made from porpoise blood mixed with oatmeal, and with forcemeats stuffed into the necks of capons.

In the mid-fourteenth century "white" puddings that replaced blood with cream and included eggs, raisins, dates, sugar, spices, suet, and pounded meat appeared. There were also Lenten puddings that eliminated the meat altogether, paving the way for the pudding as a dessert dish. Other meat-less versions were developed during the Tudor and Stuart eras, and experiments with containers other than gut were carried out with hollowed carrots, turnips, cucumbers, and cabbages. However, the most useful innovation was the pudding cloth. The pudding mixture was shaped by hand into a sphere and placed in a floured pudding cloth, which was then drawn together and knotted at the corners. This innovation meant that puddings could be made independently of slaughtered animals and conveniently boiled in the same container with another dish. One of the very first pudding cloth recipes is a set of instructions written down in 1617 for Cambridge, or college, puddings, which were served to students in the college halls. A recipe for a college pudding that does not require a pudding cloth is found in this chapter.

Elizabethan cooks also created the pudding-pie technique of baking a pudding with a pastry crust over it. This later developed into a pie with the pudding mixture put into a pastry crust. "Hasty pudding" recipes were created with pudding mixtures boiled in cooking pots, and suet pudding mixtures were formed into small balls and fried in butter. By the end of the seventeenth century the boiled pudding was usually composed of a suet crust around a pastry. Puddings, often unique to different locales, proliferated, and, as road-building improved in the eighteenth century, the special pudding recipes of stage coach inns were passed from one part of the country to another.

By the time Mrs Hudson opened the doors of 221b Baker Street to her famous lodgers there were other sweet desserts such as pies, tarts, sherbets, ice creams, and various fruit dishes served as the final course of a meal, but an essential pillar of the British diet was resting solidly upon the pudding. "Give an English man a pudding, and he shall think it a noble treat in any part of the world," a foreign visitor to London once commented. A sentiment with which Holmes and Watson would have entirely agreed. 🍎

College Puddings

"When I first came up to London I had rooms in Montague Street, just round the corner from the British Museum, and there I waited, filling in my too abundant leisure time by studying all those branches of science which might make me more efficient. Now and again cases came in my way, principally through the introduction of old, fellow-students, for during my last years at the university there was a good deal of talk there about myself and my methods ..."

THE ADVENTURE OF THE MUSGRAVE RITUAL

Most indications are that the young Sherlock spent his university years at Oxford in the early 1870s. He was a solitary student, with few social activities save boxing and fencing, and said that "his own line of study was quite distinct from that of other fellows." However, he likely dined in the college hall, and would have appreciated these traditional puddings.

Makes 8–10 small puddings

1 cup (250 mL) cake-and-pastry flour
1 tsp (5 mL) baking powder
4 medium eggs
2/3 cup (150 mL) sugar
1/2 tsp (2 mL) cinnamon
1/3 cup (75 mL) light rum

1/4 cup (50 mL) table (18%) cream
1 cup (250 mL) raisins, plumped in hot water for 30 minutes
2/3 cup (150 mL) shredded suet

Sift the flour and baking powder into a bowl. Add the eggs, sugar, and cinnamon. Beat the mixture to a smooth batter. Stir in the rum, cream, drained raisins, and suet. Spoon batter into greased muffin tins and bake at 375°F (190°C) for 30 minutes or until browned. Serve warm with Sherry Sauce.

SHERRY SAUCE

Makes about 1 1/2 cups (375 mL)

2 tbsp (25 mL) unsalted butter
1 tbsp (15 mL) all-purpose flour
1/4 cup (50 mL) sugar
1/4 tsp (1 mL) salt
1/2 cup (125 mL) medium-sweet sherry
1/2 cup (125 mL) water
4 egg yolks, well beaten

Melt the butter in a saucepan over medium heat. Add the flour and cook for 1 minute, stirring constantly. Stir in the sugar, salt, sherry, and water. Transfer to the top of a double boiler or a heatproof bowl set over a pan of boiling water. Stir in the eggs briskly, continuing to stir until the mixture thickens. Do not allow it to boil or it will curdle. Serve warm. 🍏

Iced Apple Pudding

It was a blazing hot day in August. Baker Street was like an oven, and the glare of the sunlight upon the yellow brickwork of the houses across the road was painful to the eye. It was hard to believe that these were the same walls which loomed so gloomily through the fogs of winter. Our blinds were half-drawn, and Holmes lay curled upon the sofa, reading and re-reading a letter which he had received by the morning post. For myself, my term of service in India had trained me to stand heat better than cold, and a thermometer at 90 was no hardship …

THE ADVENTURE OF THE CARDBOARD BOX

So many of Holmes's investigations seem to have taken place in chilly autumn or bitter winter months that it is hard to associate heat with them. However, we can be sure that Mrs Hudson took the prevailing weather into account in her menus, and her lodgers would have greatly appreciated this Victorian summer dessert on a hot summer's day. It is an adaptation of a recipe from Mrs Beeton's *Book of Household Management* (1861).

Serves 6

5 medium apples, peeled and sliced

2 tbsp (25 mL) apricot jam

1/3 cup (75 mL) superfine sugar

1/2 cup (125 mL) brandied cherries (or candied
   cherries softened in brandy)

1 tbsp (15 mL) orange marmalade

1 cup (250 mL) whipping (35%) cream

3 tbsp (50 mL) Cointreau or other orange liqueur

Cook the apples with the apricot jam in a covered saucepan over low heat until the apples are soft, making sure they do not burn. Purée with all but 2 tbsp (25 mL) of the sugar. Put in a bowl, stir in the cherries and marmalade, and leave to cool. Put in the freezer for 20 minutes.

Whip the cream with the remaining sugar and the Cointreau until soft peaks form. Fold it into the apple mixture. Pour into a jelly or ice cream mould and freeze.

Ten minutes before serving, dip in hot water for a few seconds, then unmould onto a serving plate. ❦

Sussex Pond Pudding

*"Rubbish, Watson, rubbish! What have we to do with walking
corpses who can only be held in their grave by stakes driven through
their hearts? It's pure lunacy ...*

*"This agency stands flat-footed upon the ground, and there it
must remain. This world is big enough for us. No 'ghosts need
apply."*

THE ADVENTURE OF THE SUSSEX VAMPIRE

*I*t took very little time for Holmes to prove that there were
merely human, and not vampire, realities at work in an investigation set in an ancient farmhouse in rural Sussex. However,
Sussex Pond Pudding is very much a reality. It was also a
Victorian favourite and is one of the more interesting of all
puddings.

Serves 6

> 2 cups (500 mL) cake-and-pastry flour
> 1 tbsp (15 mL) baking powder
> Pinch salt
> 3/4 cup (175 mL) shredded suet
> 3/4 cup (175 mL) (approx.) milk
> 3/4 cup (175 mL) unsalted butter
> 1 cup (250 mL) brown sugar
> 1 large lemon, well washed and pricked
>   all over with a skewer

Sift the flour with the baking powder and salt into a large bowl. Stir in the suet. Add enough of the milk to make a soft but not sticky dough. Knead it lightly.

On a lightly floured surface, roll out two-thirds of the dough and line the bottom and sides of a well-greased 2 1/2-pint (1.5 L) pudding basin.

Cream the butter and sugar together and put half of it in the basin. Lay in the lemon. Top with the remaining creamed mixture. Dampen the edges of the pastry. Roll out the remaining pastry and use it as a lid to cover the filling. Seal the edges well. Cover the pudding with foil with a pleat for expansion, and fasten the foil with string around the edge of the basin.

Stand the pudding in 3 inches (8 cm) of boiling water in a large pot. Cover and boil for 3 hours, adding water when it gets low. Remove the pudding from the pot, take off the foil, and run a knife around the edge of the pastry. Turn it out onto a deep serving dish that has enough room for the "pond" of lemon-flavoured melted butter and sugar that will run out when it is cut open.

Note: Occasionally a slice of the lemon is served with a portion of the pudding. However, this is entirely a matter of taste. ❦

Cabinet Pudding

"Glad to hear you have seen some light. The Cabinet awaits your final report with the utmost anxiety. Urgent representations have arrived from the very highest quarter. The whole force of the State is at your back if you should need it.

—Mycroft"

THE ADVENTURE OF THE BRUCE-PARTINGTON PLANS

*H*olmes was asked by his elder brother, Mycroft, an omnipresence in the Foreign Office whose judgement on many occasions "has decided national policy," to retrieve the stolen plans for the Bruce-Partington submarine. The involvement of the parliamentary Cabinet testified to the consequence of the matter.

Cabinet pudding (also known as chancellor's pudding) was traditional at Westminster and perhaps in less urgent moments was relished by both Sherlock and his brother.

Serves 4–6

1 tbsp (15 mL) unsalted butter or margarine
3 eggs
1/2 cup (125 mL) sugar
4 tsp (20 mL) brandy
1/2 tsp (2 mL) vanilla
Pinch salt
2/3 cup (150 mL) milk
1/2 lb (250 g) stale sponge or Madeira cake, crumbled
1/3 cup (75 mL) raisins
1/3 cup (75 mL) currants
1/4 cup (50 mL) candied, chopped cherries
1 tsp (5 mL) candied lemon peel
1 tsp (5 mL) candied orange peel

Grease the bottom and sides of a 2-pint (1.25 L) pudding basin with the butter. Beat the eggs and sugar together in a bowl. Stir in the brandy, vanilla, and salt. Lightly beat in the milk. Stir in the crumbled cake, raisins, and currants.

Sprinkle the cherries and candied peel over the bottom and sides of the pudding basin. Pour in the pudding mixture. Let stand for 2 hours. Cover with foil, leaving a pleat for expansion. Secure the foil with string under the rim of the bowl. Place in a large pot and add boiling water to come a third of the way up the side of the pudding basin. Cover and boil gently for 2 hours, replacing water when necessary. The pudding will be firm when it is done.

Serve warm with Cabinet Pudding Sauce or another sweet sauce.

CABINET PUDDING SAUCE

Makes about 1 1/2 cups (375 mL)

> 1 tbsp (15 mL) unsalted butter, softened
> 1 cup (250 mL) superfine sugar
> 5 egg yolks
> Juice of 2 medium lemons (about 2 tbsp/25 mL)
> 1/2 tsp (2 mL) grated lemon peel
> 1/4 tsp (1 mL) nutmeg
> 1/3 cup (75 mL) medium-dry sherry
> 1/2 cup (125 mL) water

In a heatproof bowl, cream the butter with the sugar. Add the egg yolks, lemon juice, lemon peel, and nutmeg. Beat with an electric beater on high for 3 minutes or until the mixture is smooth and just begins to froth. Add the sherry and water; beat for another 30 seconds. Set bowl over a pan of boiling water or transfer to a double boiler. Gently whisk the sauce until it thickens. Do not allow it to boil or the sauce will curdle. Serve warm. 🍂

Gooseberry Fool

"And now, my dear Watson, we have had some weeks of severe work, and for one evening, I think, we may turn our thoughts into more pleasant channels. I have a box for 'Les Huguenots'. Have you heard the De Reszkes? Might I trouble you then to be ready in half an hour, and we can stop at Marcini's for a little dinner on the way?"

THE HOUND OF THE BASKERVILLES

We are not informed as to the menu at Marcini's; perhaps it was Italian and similar to the Goldini's referred to in the Bruce-Partington affair. But, in any case, it would have made allowance for dessert courses known to its London clientele. Fools—combinations of puréed fruit and cream—were a popular dessert with Victorian chefs. They were attractive and much easier to make than ice cream. This recipe can be made with currants, raspberries, blackberries, or almost any other fruit. Gooseberries are tart and the sugar content can be increased if desired.

Serves 4–6

        1 lb (500 g) gooseberries
        2/3 cup (150 mL) superfine sugar
        1/4 cup (50 mL) water
        1 cup (250 mL) whipping (35%) cream

Remove any bits of stem from the gooseberries and wash them well. Put them in a saucepan with the sugar and water. Bring to a boil, then cover and let simmer for 30 minutes. Remove from the heat and mash the berries thoroughly. Press the mixture through a sieve, then chill it.

Beat the cream until it forms stiff peaks. Gently fold in the chilled purée for a marbled effect. Serve immediately in individual dishes.

Note: It can be difficult to obtain tinned gooseberries, and although they have a long season (late April to August) it may be easier to use another fresh fruit for this recipe. ❦

Irene Adler Trifle

"I only caught a glance of her at the moment, but she was a lovely woman, with a face that a man might die for."

A Scandal in Bohemia

*H*olmes used these words to describe Irene Adler, the one protagonist who actually outwitted him. He was so impressed with her intelligence and beauty that he kept a photograph of her in his rooms and, according to Dr Watson, always referred to her as *"the* woman." Irene Adler Trifle, which resembles other Victorian trifles of the day, has been created in her honour.

Serves 6

> 6 Naples or large ladyfinger biscuits
> 1/4 cup (50 mL) medium-sweet sherry
> 1/4 cup (50 mL) brandied cherries (or candied
>   cherries softened in brandy)
> 4 egg yolks
> 2 tbsp (25 mL) superfine sugar
> 2 1/2 cups (625 mL) milk

2/3 cup (150 mL) whipping (35%) cream
2 tbsp (25 mL) candied orange peel

Place the biscuits on the bottom of a glass bowl and pour the sherry over them. Spread three-quarters of the brandied cherries on top.

Make a custard by beating the egg yolks with the sugar. Heat the milk in a saucepan until warm to the touch, then slowly stir it into the yolks. Return the mixture to the pan and cook it over a low heat, stirring constantly with a wooden spoon. Do not allow it to boil. When it has thickened enough to coat the back of the spoon, pour it over the biscuits. Allow it to cool.

Beat the whipping cream to soft peaks, then spoon it over the custard. Decorate with the candied peel and remaining cherries. Serve at room temperature. 🍒

Lemon Syllabub

It was upon the 3rd of May that we reached the little village of Meiringen, where we put up at the Englischer Hof, *then kept by Peter Steiler the elder. Our landlord was an intelligent man, and spoke excellent English, having served for three years as waiter at the Grosvenor Hotel in London.*

THE ADVENTURE OF THE FINAL PROBLEM

Peter Steiler the elder must have brought some experience with cuisine as well as his facility with the language back to his inn in the Swiss Alps. A syllabub (in earlier years sillabub) was a traditional dessert that would have pleased his English guests and gone well in Alpine dairy surroundings. This recipe is for a "solid" syllabub, meaning that the cream is whipped, then the other ingredients are folded in.

Serves 6

2 cups (500 mL) whipping (35%) cream
1/3 cup (75 mL) superfine sugar
1/2 cup (125 mL) medium sherry
Juice of half a lemon (1 tbsp/15 mL)
1 tbsp (15 mL) grated lemon zest

Whip the cream in a chilled bowl, gradually adding the sugar until stiff peaks form. Fold in the sherry and lemon juice. Chill. Serve in individual glass bowls garnished with a sprinkling of lemon zest. 🦋

Christmas at Baker Street

"There are a few of us who frequent the Alpha Inn near the Museum ... This year our good host, Windigate by name, instituted a goose-club, by which, on consideration of some few pence every week, we were to receive a bird at Christmas. My pence were duly paid, and the rest is familiar to you ..."

THE ADVENTURE OF THE BLUE CARBUNCLE

 plump goose was a fundamental to many Victorians during Christmas, but in this story, the near indigent museum attendant, Henry Baker, lost his in a strange robbery involving a thief who used the bird's entrails as a hiding place for an invaluable gemstone belonging to the Countess of Morcar. Holmes not only managed to recover the gemstone, he also replaced the missing goose, an act for which Baker was extremely grateful, as, in his own words, "shillings have not been so plentiful with me as they once were," and a goose was an expensive item. Hence his membership in a goose-club, a common institution of the Victorian Christmas.

What Holmes and Watson knew as Christmas had changed much since 601, when Pope Gregory I ordered Augustine of Canterbury to deck churches in greenery and undertake

Christmas feasting as a way of displacing the winter festivals of Mithraism and other early religions competing with Christianity. By the Middle Ages, Christmastide was an elaborate twelve-day pageant of banqueting, dancing, and ceremony that began with the Nativity and ended with Epiphany on January 6. In 1642, Oliver Cromwell attempted to abolish it altogether, issuing orders to his Puritan shock troops to confiscate and burn Christmas greenery, while town criers went through the streets shouting "No Christmas! No Christmas!" The repression continued for eighteen years, ending with the coronation of Charles II.

In 1752 the calendar in England was altered and the festival was observed eleven days earlier. This led to a shortening of the holiday to Christmas Day, a change that suited the new labour demands of urban factories, which could ill afford a twelve-day halt in production. Christmas withered as a public festival, but was reborn as part of the nineteenth-century Romantic movement. This renewed interest was a protest against the loss of a "golden age" of rural tradition as well as a reaction to some of the degrading brutalities of the "dark, satanic mills" of the Industrial Revolution. Charles Dickens, who is credited as a major figure in the re-creation of Christmas for a Victorian audience, graphically described both the deplorable working conditions of the urban poor and the charms of the traditional Christmas.

Christmas culinary traditions have changed during the centuries, but many display a remarkable longevity, holding fast, if not precisely, to their histories. The goose, for example, remained a preferred Christmas bird in Baker Street and many other households during Holmes's day, although the turkey, which took its first British culinary curtain call in the sixteenth century, quickly began to put in some very popular boiled and roasted appearances. However, some of the more traditionally acclaimed fowl, such as the spectacular but rather tough peacock, and the elegant swan, both celebratory festival birds of the wealthy in the Middle Ages, had more or less lost their star billing by the seventeenth century, although swan was seen on royal Christmas Day menus until it was replaced by turkey in 1851.

Wild and tame fowl were favourite gifts during Christmastide and were often presented to manor houses by tenant farmers. One famous fowl dish, which Holmes would have been familiar with from his Yorkshire youth, was Yorkshire Christmas pie. It was extremely popular during the eighteenth century and was a direct descendant of the enormous pies of the Middle Ages. It included the flesh of a turkey, a goose, a chicken, a partridge, a pigeon, a hare, and a number of woodcocks and moor game, all well seasoned and baked in a thick crust with several pounds of butter. It was often sent to London as a present for relatives.

That other centrepiece of the holiday table, the plum pudding, had its origin in the fifteenth century as a stewed winter broth. By the Elizabethan period it was a Christmas pottage made with meat, herbs, breadcrumbs, dried fruit, and spices. The adaptation of the pudding cloth in the seventeenth century enabled it to be cooked as a solid dessert, the meat ingredients were eventually removed, and by the eighteenth century it was usually laced with claret and sack. It was a royal favourite of the Hanover King George I, who was delighted with it when it was served to him on the evening of December 25, 1714, his first British Christmas. Its merits were later promoted by another royal figure of German origin, the Saxe-Coburg Prince Albert of Christmas tree fame, who married Queen Victoria in 1840.

In 1843 Charles Dickens's *A Christmas Carol* appeared on the stands with a description of the Cratchit family's Christmas dinner. Their plum pudding, "regarded by Bob Cratchit as the greatest success achieved by Mrs Cratchit since their marriage," is pictured as "a speckled cannon-ball, so hard and firm, blazing in half of half-a-quartern of ignited brandy, and bedight with Christmas holly stuck into the top." Holmes may or may not have read Dickens's works, but he would have been well acquainted with Christmas pudding. There can be no question that puddings were part of Mrs Hudson's Christmas menus, along with black bun, a traditional rich Scottish Christmas bun Watson would have been quite familiar with. Shortbread, which by that time was well known as a particularly Scottish Christmas treat, and often sent as a festival present to English friends and relatives, was no doubt one of her specialties. She would have also made mince pies, once known as shred pies because of the shredded meat that was mixed with dried fruits, sugar, and spices. They were already Christmas fare in Elizabethan days. Sweet dried fruits such as plums, currants, figs, and dates were valued in pies because of the expense of sugar. As in puddings, the meat ingredients were abandoned over time—some Victorian recipes still require beef as part of mincemeat—but the dried fruits remained in Christmas pies, puddings, and cakes even when sugar became less costly and was easily available.

Mrs Hudson's Christmas kitchen must have also benefited from the Gallic influence on Scottish cuisine that followed the "auld alliance" of Scotland and France and the passion that Mary Queen of Scots, who ruled Scotland from 1561 to 1568, had for French cooking. Holmes, whose grandmother was French, and who was entirely fluent in the language, would have appreciated such items as the Christmas chestnut cake, which is found in the recipes of this chapter.

One traditional specialty that had been Christmas fare since the Middle Ages but that probably didn't appear at 221b was brawn, a rich and fatty dish made of the head and foreparts of a boar or pig. It was occasionally mentioned in Victorian Christmas menus, but had largely fallen out of favour by Holmes's day. Yet the annual tradition of bringing in a boar's head on a platter to the accompaniment of the "Boar's Head Carol" in Queen's College, Oxford, remains to this day, and Holmes may have witnessed it during his university days.

We can be assured, however, that nothing was stinted on the festive "groaning board" at Baker Street and that Holmes and Watson were well fêted by Mrs Hudson. There is evidence of that even two days after Christmas when Holmes, at the close of the Blue Carbuncle affair, says, "If you will have the goodness to touch the bell, Doctor, we will begin another investigation, in which also a bird will be the chief factor," and they both sat down to enjoy a delicious meal of roast woodcock. 🐦

Baker Street Christmas Goose with Prune Stuffing

"A most unimpeachable Christmas goose."

THE ADVENTURE OF THE BLUE CARBUNCLE

This was how Holmes described the Christmas goose of Henry Baker, the unfortunate individual who was assaulted by a "knot of roughs" on Christmas morning and lost his treasured bird.

A goose can make a delightful change to the standard Christmas turkey fare, but it is usually a fatty bird and must be cooked properly. Geese also can be quite tough when fully mature, and for this reason it is best to buy one that is no heavier than 12 lb (5.5 kg).

Serves 4–6

1 goose (8–12 lb/3.5–5.5 kg)

PRUNE STUFFING
3/4 lb (375 g) pitted prunes
2 cups (500 mL) fresh brown breadcrumbs
1 1/2 cups (375 mL) chopped fresh parsley
1 tbsp (15 mL) chopped fresh thyme
1 1/2 tsp (7 mL) salt
1/2 tsp (2 mL) pepper
1 egg, beaten

Chop the prunes into small pieces, then mix with breadcrumbs, parsley, thyme, salt, pepper, and egg. Stuff the goose and seal the cavity with skewers or thread. Place the goose on a rack in a roasting pan and roast at 400°F (200°C) for 30 minutes. Prick the skin all over with a skewer, making sure not to prick the flesh.

Reduce heat to 350°F (180°C) and roast the goose for another 30 minutes. Pour away half of the fat in the pan. Prick the skin all over again and return goose to oven. Cook until tender, for a total of 20 minutes per pound. (The total cooking time, which includes the initial 1 hour, will be between 2 1/2 and 4 hours.)

Serve with roast potatoes and a green vegetable. ❦

Christmas Spiced Beef

I had called upon my friend Sherlock Holmes upon the second morning after Christmas, with the intention of wishing him the compliments of the season.

THE ADVENTURE OF THE BLUE CARBUNCLE

One of the dishes Holmes and Watson would have looked forward to during yuletide was spiced beef, traditionally served on one of the latter twelve days of Christmas. It is a simple recipe, but requires about two weeks of marination.

Serves 10 as an appetizer

> 2 lb (1 kg) topside of beef
> 1/2 cup (125 mL) dark brown sugar
> 1/2 cup (125 mL) coarse salt
> 1 tbsp (15 mL) white pepper
> 1 tbsp (15 mL) black peppercorns
> 2 tsp (10 mL) turmeric
> 2 tsp (10 mL) allspice
> 3/4 cup (175 mL) water

Trim any fat from the beef. Place it in a large casserole dish and rub the brown sugar into the meat. Rub in the salt. Mix together the white pepper, peppercorns, turmeric, and allspice. Press all over the meat. Cover the dish and put it in the refrigerator. Turn the beef over once a day for 12 days, pressing into the meat any loose spices, salt, or sugar.

On the twelfth day, run the beef under cold water to remove any spices, salt, and sugar. Return the beef to the casserole and add 3/4 cup (175 mL) of water. Cover and bake at 275°F (140°C) for 3 1/2 hours or until the meat is tender.

Cool to room temperature and wrap in foil. Place a flat plate on it and put a 3–4 lb (1.5–2 kg) weight such as a frying pan on the plate. Refrigerate overnight.

Carve the beef into thin slices. It will keep, wrapped in foil and refrigerated, 3–4 weeks.

Note: Be sure to use coarse salt. A fine grade of salt will be absorbed in the meat, affecting the flavour. Coarse salt is sometimes sold as "kosher" salt. 🐝

Black Bun

I had neither kith nor kin in England, and was therefore as free as air—or as free as an income of eleven shillings and sixpence a day will permit a man to be.

A STUDY IN SCARLET

*D*r Watson said this after his return from India and some Sherlockians have cited it as evidence of his Scottish origins. Perhaps in his youth he even encountered that raconteur of investigative tales, Sir Arthur Conan Doyle, who left Edinburgh to further his medical career in England.

In any case, Watson was likely quite familiar with black bun, or Scotch Christmas bun as it is also known. It was traditionally baked for Hogmanay and Twelfth Night, and it should be kept at least ten days before it is eaten. It is very rich in taste and can be stored for up to six months in an airtight tin.

Makes one 9-inch (23 cm) round bun

PASTRY: 3 cups (750 mL) cake-and-pastry flour
1 tsp (5 mL) baking powder
Pinch salt
3/4 cup (175 mL) unsalted butter
Cold water

FILLING: 1 1/2 cups (375 mL) all-purpose flour
2 tsp (10 mL) cinnamon
1 tsp (5 mL) baking powder
1 tsp (5 mL) ginger
1 tsp (5 mL) cloves
2 1/2 cups (625 mL) raisins, plumped in hot water
for 30 minutes
2 1/2 cups (625 mL) currants, plumped in hot

water for 30 minutes
1 cup (250 mL) chopped blanched almonds
1 cup (250 mL) brown sugar
1/2 cup (125 mL) mixed candied peel
1/4 cup (50 mL) dark rum
2 tbsp (25 mL) (approx.) milk (optional)
1 egg yolk, beaten with a little water

Line the bottom and sides of a 9-inch (1.5 L) round cake pan with greased baking paper. To make the pastry, sift the flour with the baking powder and salt into a bowl. Rub in the butter. Add enough cold water to make a fairly stiff dough. Let the dough sit for an hour. Set aside one-quarter of the pastry. On a lightly floured surface, roll out remaining pastry to 1/8-inch (3 mm) thickness and line the bottom and sides of the cake pan.

To make the filling, sift together in a large bowl the flour, cinnamon, baking powder, ginger, and cloves. In another bowl mix the drained raisins and currants, almonds, brown sugar, and peel. Stir in the rum. Knead the fruit mixture into the flour. Its consistency should be thick and slightly sticky. Add the milk only if it is necessary to further bind the ingredients.

Put the mixture into the pastry-lined pan and moisten the edges of the pastry. Roll out the remaining pastry and use it as a lid, crimping the edges to thoroughly seal them together. With a skewer make four holes down to the bottom of the bun and prick all over the top with a fork. Brush with the eggwash. Bake at 325°F (160°C) for 3 hours. Let cool in the cake tin. Store, tightly covered, until required.

Note: The sweetness of different raisins and currants can vary considerably. It is wise to taste the fruit mixture and add a little more sugar if needed. ❦

Blue Carbuncle Mince Pies

"... It is the season of forgiveness. Chance has put in our way a most singular and whimsical problem, and its solution is its own reward."

THE ADVENTURE OF THE BLUE CARBUNCLE

Holmes made this statement after releasing to his freedom James Ryder, the Cosmopolitan Hotel attendant and thief of the Countess of Morcar's Blue Carbuncle. Perhaps his unusual bonhomie was aided by Mrs Hudson's seasonal cooking, of which these mince pies would be fine examples.

Makes about 24 small mince pies

FILLING
2 cups (500 mL) brown sugar
2 cups (500 mL) coarsely grated peeled apple
2 cups (500 mL) mixed light and dark raisins, finely chopped
1 1/2 cups (375 mL) currants, finely chopped
1 cup (250 mL) candied fruit peel, finely chopped
1 cup (250 mL) shredded suet
1/2 cup (125 mL) chopped blanched almonds
1/2 cup (125 mL) brandy or dark rum
2 tbsp (25 mL) grated orange zest
1 tbsp (15 mL) grated lemon zest

1 tsp (5 mL) cinnamon
1 tsp (5 mL) cloves
1/2 tsp (2 mL) nutmeg
1/2 tsp (2 mL) ginger
1/2 tsp (2 mL) salt

PASTRY
4 cups (1 L) cake-and-pastry flour
1/2 tsp (2 mL) salt
1 1/2 cups (375 mL) shortening, cut in small pieces
Cold water

Icing sugar

In a large bowl stir together well the sugar, apple, raisins, currants, candied peel, suet, almonds, brandy, orange zest, lemon zest, cinnamon, cloves, nutmeg, ginger, and salt. Cover and refrigerate for two days, stirring occasionally.

To make the pastry, sift the flour and salt into a bowl. Rub in the shortening evenly. Add enough cold water to make a fairly stiff dough. Let the dough relax for an hour. Roll out the dough to 1/8-inch (3 mm) thickness. Cut out twenty-four 3-inch (8 cm) rounds and twenty-four 2-inch (5 cm) rounds. Line greased muffin or tartlet tins with the larger circles. Spoon in the mincemeat. Moisten the edges of the pastry and cover with the smaller rounds, crimping to seal the edges. Make a hole in the centre of each and bake at 400°F (200°C) for about 20 minutes. Remove from tins and cool on a rack. Dust with icing sugar before serving. ❦

Chestnut Cake with Drambuie Icing

... The sticky spear-heads of the chestnuts were just beginning to burst into their five-fold leaves.

THE ADVENTURE OF THE YELLOW FACE

*T*his chestnut cake is a Christmas offering that may have passed down through the generations of Holmes's Gallic ancestors to his childhood. Perhaps he introduced it to Mrs Hudson, although she may have already known of it via some of the French influences on Scottish cuisine that date back to the sixteenth century. It is a very rich French cake and should be served in small slices.

Serves 8–10

> 3/4 cup (175 mL) unsalted butter
> 1 1/2 cups (375 mL) superfine sugar
> 1 1/2 cups (375 mL) unsweetened chestnut purée
> 6 eggs, separated
> 3 tbsp (50 mL) rum
> 1/2 tsp (2 mL) vanilla
> 1 cup (250 mL) cake-and-pastry flour
> 2 tsp (10 mL) baking powder
> 1 tsp (5 mL) cinnamon

Cream the butter with 1 1/4 cups (300 mL) of the sugar in a bowl. Beat in the chestnut purée. Beat in the egg yolks, one at a time. Stir in the rum and vanilla. Sift together the flour, baking powder, and cinnamon. Beat into the batter.

Beat the egg whites with the remaining sugar until stiff peaks form. Beat one-quarter of the egg whites into the chestnut batter to lighten it. Gently fold in the rest of the egg whites.

Bake in a greased 10-inch (4 L) tube pan at 375°F (190°C) for 40 minutes or until a toothpick comes out clean. Turn onto a rack to cool, then ice with Drambuie Icing.

DRAMBUIE ICING

2 tbsp (25 mL) butter, melted
2 cups (500 mL) icing sugar
3 tbsp (50 mL) Drambuie
Hot water

Stir the melted butter into the sugar. Stir in the Drambuie. Blend in enough hot water, a teaspoon at a time, to make a smooth paste. Spread over the top of the chestnut cake. ❦

Mrs Hudson's
Best-Ever Shortbread

Billy swung open the door and Inspector MacDonald of Scotland Yard was ushered into the room.

He was a silent, precise man, with a dour nature and a hard Aberdonian accent.

Twice already in his career had Holmes helped him to attain success, his own sole reward being the intellectual joy of the problem. For this reason the affection and respect of the Scotchman for his amateur colleague were profound, and he showed them by the frankness with which he consulted Holmes in every difficulty.

THE VALLEY OF FEAR

*H*olmes's consulting career was well established by the time Inspector MacDonald superseded Lestrade as the main representative of Scotland Yard to come calling at Baker Street. Perhaps the delicious odours of fine Scottish baking added to his anticipation of his encounters with the Great Detective. MacDonald would have greatly appreciated Mrs Hudson's shortbread, something that must have figured large at Baker Street during the Christmas season and at Hogmanay.

The basics of successful shortbread baking are no different now than they were in Mrs Hudson's day. The type of wheat flour used should have a low gluten content, otherwise the product will be too hard. Cake-and-pastry flour is generally used and some rice flour can be added to give a slightly crunchier shortbread. The sugar should be very fine in its granulation. This can be purchased as superfine sugar, or you may simply put regular granulated sugar in a food processor to achieve a similar result. The butter should be unsalted. Almonds in some form are

150

traditionally added to festive shortbreads and provide an extra richness of taste.

Makes 15–30 2-inch (5 cm) rounds, depending upon the desired thickness

> 1 cup (250 mL) unsalted butter, softened
> 1 cup (250 mL) superfine sugar
> 1 cup (250 mL) ground almonds
> 2 1/2 cups (625 mL) cake-and-pastry flour
> 1/2 cup (125 mL) rice flour

Knead the butter and sugar together. Mix in the ground almonds thoroughly. Sift together the cake-and-pastry flour and rice flour. Gradually knead the flour into the butter. Aim for pliable dough that is not too soft. (The moisture contents of different flours and butters can vary considerably.) Do not allow the dough to become dry to the point of breaking up. Add a little water if it is too dry and more cake-and-pastry flour if it is too moist.

On a lightly floured surface roll out the dough to a 1/4-inch (5 mm) thickness and cut into 2-inch (5 cm) rounds. Arrange on a baking sheet and prick all over with a fork to let the steam escape from the dough. Bake in the middle of the oven at 325°F (160°C) for 12–18 minutes, until just beginning to brown. Transfer to a rack and sprinkle with superfine sugar. Add another 5–10 minutes for 1/2-inch (1 cm) thick rounds. Store the shortbread in tins or plastic tubs with tight-fitting lids.

Note: Almond paste may be used instead of ground almonds. Use 1/3 cup (75 mL). Reduce the sugar used to 2/3 cup (150 mL). Cream the almond paste with the sugar before mixing it with the butter. ❦

Six Napoleons Plum Pudding

Next instant, with a loud shout of triumph, he held up one splinter, in which a round, dark object was fixed like a plum in a pudding.

"Gentlemen," he cried, "let me introduce you to the famous black pearl of the Borgias!"

THE ADVENTURE OF THE SIX NAPOLEONS

*I*n this investigation Holmes managed to recover a stolen black pearl hidden in a plaster bust of Napoleon. Watson's comparison of it to a plum in a pudding is interesting, but not entirely correct. There are very few, if any, Victorian recipes for puddings that use plums, and even the plum in the famous ditty involving little Jack Horner is misleading. Jack Horner was really the steward to the Abbot of Glastonbury, who ordered him to carry a pie to King Henry VIII in London. The pie actually contained the title deeds to twelve manors in Somerset, and was intended as a bribe to forestall the seizure of church lands by the Crown. En route Horner opened the pie and removed one of the deeds. The king took the church's land in any case, but Horner's stolen property (his "plum") remained in his family for many years.

This recipe does not require pearls, plums, or title deeds, but it does produce a very fine Christmas pudding.

Serves 8–10

> 1 1/2 cups (375 mL) mixed light and dark raisins,
>   plumped in hot water for 30 minutes
> 1 1/2 cups (375 mL) currants, plumped in hot water
>   for 30 minutes
> 3/4 cup (175 mL) mixed candied peel

3/4 cup (175 mL) finely chopped almonds
1 tsp (5 mL) grated lemon zest
1 tsp (5 mL) grated orange zest
1 1/2 cups (375 mL) shredded suet
2 cups (500 mL) dark brown sugar
1 1/2 cups (375 mL) fresh breadcrumbs
1 1/2 cups (375 mL) all-purpose flour
1 tbsp (15 mL) allspice
1/2 tsp (2 mL) salt
4 large eggs
1/3 cup (75 mL) brandy

Combine the drained raisins and currants, candied peel, almonds, lemon zest, orange zest, and suet in a bowl and mix well. Stir in the sugar, breadcrumbs, flour, allspice, and salt.

In a separate bowl beat the eggs and stir in the brandy. Pour over the fruit. Knead by hand to mix everything thoroughly. Cover and refrigerate overnight.

Put into a greased 3-pint (1.75 L) pudding basin. Cover with buttered foil, leaving a pleat for expansion. Tie the foil under the ridge of the bowl with string. Place the bowl in a large pot of boiling water that comes two-thirds of the way up the sides. Reduce the heat, cover, and boil gently for 8 hours. Replenish the water when necessary.

Cool the pudding in the basin. Remove the foil and re-cover the pudding with a fresh piece. Store at least 3 weeks before serving. The pudding can be kept up to a year in the refrigerator or in a cool place.

To serve, steam the pudding for 2 hours. Run a knife around the edge of the pudding and unmould onto a plate. To serve the pudding aflame, pour 2 tbsp (25 mL) of brandy over it and light it at the table. Or, warm the brandy in a saucepan, ignite it, and pour it over the pudding. Accompany the pudding with Brandy Butter or Cumberland Rum Butter.

BRANDY BUTTER

Makes about 3/4 cup (175 mL)

> 1/2 cup (125 mL) unsalted butter, softened
> 2/3 cup (150 mL) superfine sugar
> 3 tbsp (50 mL) brandy
> 1/2 tsp (2 mL) vanilla
> 1 tsp (2 mL) grated orange zest

Cream the butter, then beat in the sugar a few tablespoons at a time until light and fluffy. Beat in the brandy and vanilla. Mix in the orange zest. Leave in a cool place until firm.

CUMBERLAND RUM BUTTER

Traditionally served with plum pudding.

Makes about 1 cup (250 L)

> 1/2 cup (125 mL) unsalted butter, softened
> 1/2 cup (125 mL) brown sugar
> 1/4 cup (50 mL) light rum
> 1/4 tsp (1 mL) cinnamon

Cream the butter, then beat in the sugar a few tablespoons at a time until light and fluffy. Beat in the rum and cinnamon. Leave in a cool place until firm.

Note: Both these sauces are "hard" sauces and are spread on pudding with a knife and left to melt. 🍎

Port Wine Jelly

"One evening, shortly after my arrival, we were sitting over a glass of port after dinner, when young Trevor began to talk about those habits of observation and inference which I had already formed into a system, although I had not yet appreciated the part which they were to play in my life."

THE ADVENTURE OF THE "GLORIA SCOTT"

An after-dinner glass of port was always appreciated by men such as Holmes and Watson, but it was also used to make a much-loved jelly during Christmas week. The Victorians often classified jellies as "invalid cookery" because of their comparative digestive lightness, and port wine jelly was likely a welcome relief in the midst of the heavier seasonal surfeit of puddings and mince pies.

Serves 4

> 2 envelopes unflavoured gelatin (2 tbsp/25 mL)
> 1/4 cup (50 mL) water
> 2 cups (500 mL) port
> 1/2 cup (125 mL) superfine sugar
> 1/2 tsp (2 mL) cinnamon
> 2 cups (500 mL) purple grape juice

Sprinkle the gelatin over the water in a small bowl without stirring it and let it sit for 3 minutes. Meanwhile, bring the port nearly to a boil, then add the gelatin, stirring until it is dissolved. Add the sugar and cinnamon, stirring until it is dissolved. Let cool, then stir in the grape juice. Pour it into individual jelly moulds or sherry glasses that have been rinsed with cold water. Chill until firm (about 4 hours). ❦

155

Beverages

t was not unusual for Sherlock Holmes and Dr Watson to sit on either side of their sitting-room fireplace with whisky and soda at hand while Holmes unraveled the intricacies of an investigation before his astonished friend. In this instance he was successfully commissioned to discover the missing bride of one of the country's more prominent men. Whisky was usually in good supply in Baker Street, as it was in many middle- and upper-middle-class households in those days, although its origins were of a more humble order. Its distillation was initially a family affair among Lowland Scots who used surplus farm barley, burn water, a pot-still, and a peat fire to produce their own malt whisky, or *usquebagh*, which was then consumed locally or sold in nearby towns.

During the seventeenth century its distillation spread northward to the Highlands, where it became a favourite with the poor, who often drank it from scallop shells they carried about with them. The popular liquor among the Scottish gentry was French brandy, although whisky became the basic ingredient in toddies and other famous drinks such as the celebrated Atholl brose and het pint, both of which would have been well known to Mrs Hudson, and are featured in the recipes of this chapter.

The earliest of alcoholic beverages in Britain, mead—a fermented honey and water concoction—was generally out of fashion by Holmes's day. At one time a warrior's drink consumed by the Celtic and Saxon aristocracy, it continued to be popular in some parts of the country until the eighteenth century. Ale and beer, on the other hand—of which a Celtic barley variation was noted by classical writers after Pytheas, the Greek explorer, circumnavigated Britain in 300 BC—have never lost their appeal. Ale, brewed from wheat, oats, or barley, was the principal drink among ordinary folk during the Anglo-Saxon and Norman periods and up through the Middle Ages, until it was challenged in the fifteenth century by the hopped version known as beer, which was drunk at all times of the day, from breakfast to the late evening hours.

Most of the wines available to Holmes and Watson came from France and Germany, although cheap sugar from the colonies gave rise to local wines made from grapes and other fruits commonly available. Wine was first brought to Europe in the seventh century BC by Greek colonists in Marseilles, who eventually traded it across northern France and the Rhineland. It reached southeast England several decades before the Romans introduced their own viticulture in Britain in the years following their invasion in AD 43. The Roman vineyards languished after they left, but were substantially revived by the monasteries. Later, native wine production collapsed with the confiscation of church lands in the Tudor era, and by Elizabethan times most wine in Britain was imported. The consumption of sack, or Spanish wine, became common, and port—Portuguese wine fortified with brandy—took hold in the early eighteenth century and became increasingly popular onward as relations with France worsened. Holmes and Watson often availed themselves of a glass of port after a fine meal.

The process of spirit distillation, first employed by apothecaries and monks to create medicines, was taken over by professional distillers of rye and corn spirit in Europe in the fourteenth century. Later, Elizabethan soldiers returning from the Dutch wars brought back with them their taste for the juniper-flavoured corn spirit known as genever or gin. In 1638 the Company of Distillers was incorporated in London and given control over the trade of distilled spirits. However, parliamentary acts introduced in 1690 and 1790 encouraged home-produced corn spirit and spirits of cider in an attempt to curb smuggling and reduce imports of French brandy. Gin shops of the "drunk for a penny; dead drunk for two-pence; clean straw for nothing" variety proliferated, and crude, cheap, but powerful spirits began to wreak the social havoc among the urban poor so eloquently depicted by Hogarth. Successive tax increases on distilled spirits throughout the eighteenth century reduced some of the worst excesses, but drunkenness among the urban poor remained a grave social problem during Holmes's era.

A much more benign form of beverage, particularly characteristic of the Victorian period, can be found in cookbooks of the day in chapters about invalid cookery. These usually included recipes for such items as barley water, beef tea, and various mutton, calf's foot, eel, and chicken broth drinks for people who were being nursed back to health. Dr Watson would likely have prescribed them to many of his patients. Two examples of these are given in this chapter.

The traditional nonalcoholic beverages in England were milk, buttermilk, whey, and water, although the introduction of chocolate, coffee, and tea in the seventeenth century had a considerable effect on the drinking habits of society. The first coffee house in the country was established in Oxford in 1650; from there they spread to London, where coffee became fashionable among the upper and middle classes. Drinking chocolate became popular about the same time; chocolate houses proliferated, and coffee and chocolate became preferred gentry breakfast drinks during the eighteenth century.

Tea from China, via Dutch traders in Java and Sumatra, also made its first appearance in England in the 1650s. Although it was expensive, Catherine, the Portuguese wife of Charles II, encouraged its use at Court, and the East India Company shipped increasing amounts into the country, along with the fine porcelain cups and teapots central to the culture of tea consumption. By the end of the century 20 million pounds, or two pounds per head, of tea was being imported on an annual basis. It was estimated that the same amount again was smuggled into the country. Thomas Twining opened a tea shop for ladies in 1717, and tea gardens, as they were later known, were open to the general public, spreading the new drinking habit among all classes.

The stronger teas of India and Ceylon replaced the Chinese varieties in the nineteenth century, and by Holmes's day tea, often without milk or sugar, had become the regular stimulant of the working class. This has been decried by some commentators on the Victorian diet, who have pointed out that the consumption of the hot fluid provided a deceptive sense of well-being, and that it was often used to replace more nutritious food. It was also an inadequate substitute for the beer used as a daily beverage among the poor of earlier generations. By this time coffee houses had disappeared and there was a sharp decline in sales of drinking chocolate and coffee. However, tea does not seem to have had an impact at Baker Street. "There's coffee on the table, Watson, and I have a cab at the door," Holmes says early one morning in *The Adventure of the Six Napoleons*, and there are frequent references to coffee as the standard breakfast beverage set out at 221b. But then, perhaps the ever-patient Mrs Hudson was simply catering to another of the many eccentricities of her much-acclaimed lodger. ❦

Baked Beef Tea

On referring to my notes, I see that it was on the 14th of April that I received a telegram from Lyons, which informed me that Holmes was lying ill in the Hotel Dulong. Within twenty-four hours I was in his sick room, and was relieved to find that there was nothing formidable in his symptoms. His iron constitution, however, had broken down under the strain of an investigation ...

THE ADVENTURE OF THE REIGATE SQUIRE

Although Holmes had overcome the "colossal schemes of Baron Maupertuis," the most accomplished swindler in Europe, and his room was "ankle-deep with congratulatory telegrams," he was clearly exhausted. A concerned Watson brought him back first to Baker Street, and then on to the house of his friend Colonel Hayter, near Reigate in Surrey. Holmes was soon called upon to take up another case, but in the meantime he rested, and there can be little doubt that his convalescent regime included beef tea, a well-known "fortifying drink" served to Victorian patients who were recovering their health.

Makes about 4 cups (1 L)

1 lb (500 g) stewing beef
1/2 medium onion, sliced
1 tbsp (15 mL) butter

4 cups (1 L) water
1/2 tsp (2 mL) salt
1 whole clove

Remove any fat from the beef. In a large frying pan, fry the onion lightly in butter, then add the beef and brown it on all sides. Put the meat in a casserole dish with the water, salt, and clove. Cover and bake at 350°F (180°C) for 2 hours.

Cool, then skim off any fat. Strain the tea and drink at room temperature or reheated. It will keep for about a week in the refrigerator.

Note: In Victorian days the leftover beef from beef tea was sometimes pounded into potted beef, but it is unlikely to be particularly useful to the contemporary cook. ❦

Atholl Brose

The yellow glare from the shop-windows streamed out into the
steamy, vaporous air, and threw a murky, shifting radiance across
the crowded thoroughfare. There was, to my mind, something eerie
and ghost-like in the endless procession of faces which flitted across
these narrow bars of light ... I am not subject to impressions, but
the dull, heavy evening, with the strange business upon which we
were engaged, combined to make me nervous and depressed.

THE SIGN OF FOUR

Mrs Hudson, sensing Watson's despondency, might well have offered him some of her own Atholl brose, an old Scottish drink supposedly developed by the Earl of Atholl during a Highland rebellion in 1475. The legend has it that the earl filled his enemies' wells with the mixture and it made them so pleasantly drunk that he captured them easily. A tumblerful would have surely lifted Watson's spirits!

Makes 4 cups (1 L)

> 1 1/2 cups (375 mL) quick-cooking oatmeal
> 2 1/2 cups (625 mL) water
> 1/2 cup (125 mL) honey
> Whisky

Mix the oatmeal with water and leave it to stand for 30 minutes. Strain through a fine sieve. Stir the honey into the oatmeal water, then pour it into a 1-quart (1 L) bottle or jar. Add whisky to fill and seal the bottle. Shake well before using.

Atholl brose will keep for several months in a liquor cabinet. 🐦

Barley Water

I was so weak and emaciated that a medical board determined that not a day should be lost in sending me back to England. I was dispatched, accordingly, in the troopship Orontes, *and landed a month later on Portsmouth Jetty, with my health irretrievably ruined, but with permission from a paternal government to spend the next nine months in attempting to improve it.*

A STUDY IN SCARLET

𝒟r Watson arrived in Portsmouth in late November of 1880, several weeks before he was to meet Sherlock Holmes. During this period he probably became quite familiar with the drink barley water. It is a very soothing beverage for anyone in a weakened condition.

Makes about 4 cups (1 L)

> 1/3 cup (75 mL) pearl barley
> 10 cups (2.5 L) water
> Juice of 1 lemon (2 tbsp/25 mL)
> Sugar to taste

Rinse the barley with cold water, then put it into a saucepan, add 2 cups (500 mL) of the water, and bring to a boil. Let it boil for 3 minutes, then drain. Bring the remaining 8 cups (2 L) of water to a boil in a large pot, add the barley, and simmer until the liquid is reduced by half. Strain the liquid and stir the lemon juice into it. Add sugar to taste. Store the barley water in a sealed bottle; it will keep up to 4 days in the refrigerator. ❦

Het Pint

In a quarter of an hour we were in Bloomsbury at the Alpha Inn, which is a small public-house at the corner of one of the streets which runs down into Holborn. Holmes pushed open the door of the private bar and ordered two glasses of beer from the ruddy-faced, white-aproned landlord.

THE ADVENTURE OF THE BLUE CARBUNCLE

Holmes and Watson were never averse to a glass of ale or beer, in this instance as a preliminary to questioning the Alpha Inn landlord as to his source of Christmas geese. The Blue Carbuncle affair was concluded on December 27, and five days later Mrs Hudson may have offered her two lodgers het pint, an ale-based beverage traditionally served on New Year's morning and on the night before a wedding in the Scottish Borders.

Makes 7–8 cups (1.75–2 L)

2 medium eggs
6 cups (1.5 L) pale ale
1/2 tsp (2 mL) nutmeg
2 tbsp (25 mL) sugar
3/4 cup (175 mL) whisky

Beat the eggs in a large bowl and set aside. Pour the ale into a saucepan and stir in the nutmeg. Heat to nearly boiling, stir in the sugar, and remove from heat. Stir 1/4 cup (50 mL) of the hot liquid into the eggs. Stir in the rest of the liquid slowly, stirring constantly. Stir in the whisky and return the mixture to the saucepan. Heat to near the boiling point, stirring constantly. Do not allow it to boil. Pour into a drinking tankard and pour the "het" pint back and forth between the saucepan and tankard until a froth forms. Serve at once. 🍎

Claret Cup

We had a pleasant little meal together, during which Holmes would talk about nothing but violins … This led him to Paganini, and we sat for an hour over a bottle of claret while he told me anecdote after anecdote of that extraordinary man. The afternoon was far advanced and the hot glare had softened into a mellow glow before we found ourselves at the police-station. Lestrade was waiting for us at the door.

THE ADVENTURE OF THE CARDBOARD BOX

*T*he bottle of claret Holmes and Watson shared on a hot August afternoon may have on other occasions been used in claret cup, a refreshing Victorian drink on warm-weather days.

> 1 bottle (26 oz/750 mL) claret (red Bordeaux)
> 1/4 cup (50 mL) superfine sugar
> 1/4 cup (50 mL) Maraschino or other cherry-flavoured
>   liqueur
> 1/4 tsp (1 mL) nutmeg
> 6 whole cloves
> 6 fresh mint leaves
> 1 sprig borage or a few slices of cucumber rind
> Club soda
> Ice

Put all the ingredients except the club soda and ice into a large bowl. Stir until the sugar dissolves, then let stand for 30 minutes. Strain into a large bottle or jar and seal. It will keep indefinitely in the refrigerator.

To use, half fill a wine glass with soda water, then add the claret mixture and an ice cube. ❦

Sauces and Preserves

Some weeks afterwards I learned incidentally that my friend spent a day at Windsor, whence he returned with a remarkably fine emerald tie-pin. When I asked him if he had bought it, he answered that it was a present from a certain gracious lady in whose interests he had been fortunate enough to carry out a small commission.

THE ADVENTURE OF THE BRUCE-PARTINGTON PLANS

olmes's detective talents were well known to the Queen and he was received at Buckingham Palace and Windsor several times for private conferences on matters of state and personal concerns of the royal family. There is no doubt that he was invited to dine there as well, and it would be fascinating to know what was set before him. Some excellent chefs spent time in royal service, Charles Francatelli being one of them. Francatelli spent a year at Buckingham Palace when Queen Victoria was still young, before moving on to several other noble households and the Reform Club. He had left the palace well before Holmes's time, but his influence lingered. Like all great chefs, he put considerable emphasis on sauces, stating in his book *The Modern Cook* (1846) that their preparation demanded "great care and watchful attention." The béchamel sauce in this chapter is a variation on a

Francatelli recipe. It serves well as a base for many other sauces, and would have been present in any of the multi-course royal banquets Holmes might have attended.

Holmes may have also sampled some of the chutneys that were offered with the Indian dishes at the palace. Part of the Queen's household was given over to Indian cooks who prepared their own chutneys and ground all their own curry spices between two large stones on the palace grounds. Chutney (from the Hindustani *chatni*, meaning strong, sweet relish) was popular throughout the realm, particularly with those who had toiled in the service of Victoria's Raj. The recipe for Dr Watson's Favourite Chutney has been created in honour of the doctor's efforts as an assistant surgeon during the second Afghan campaign.

Most of the other fish and meat sauces of Holmes's day were derived from the leftover pickling liquor found in ketchups, which had their origins in the *koe-chiap*, pickled fish sauces of the Orient, and the highly seasoned vinegars used in making Piccalilli-type pickled vegetable mixtures. Variations of these, such as Harvey's Sauce and Lea and Perrins Worcestershire Sauce (originally known as Lord Sandy's Sauce), were retailed by a few London grocers in the eighteenth century. By the next century bottled sauces were widely available in most households and a number of dining establishments. Oyster bars and reasonably priced chop-houses, such as the well-known Keen's in Holborn, offered a large choice of commercial condiments. Keen's was not too far from St Bart's Hospital, where Holmes was studying analytical chemistry and anatomy when he first met Watson in January of 1881. Both of them were low on funds in those days and were probably quite familiar with Keen's and other chop-houses.

It is worth noting that the Victorian sauces Holmes and

Watson knew, although not as potent as the earlier medieval spice preparations intended as disguises for tainted meats, were usually far more piquant than their modern counterparts, and probably served as useful antidotes to some of the unappetizing, fatty, and coarse-grained imported tinned beef that was new on the market at that time.

Sweet sauces and preserves had also taken on a new character in the late Victorian era. What has come to be familiar to us as jam—that concoction made by bruising, then boiling soft fruit in sugar—became increasingly well known during the latter part of the eighteenth century. Its growth in popularity was in part due to the cheaper sugar imported from the colonies, and by the nineteenth century jam making was common in middle-class households. The blackcurrant jam featured in this chapter is a fine example of what Mrs Hudson might have prepared in her kitchen.

Jam eventually replaced the "fruit solids" of earlier generations that were made by cooking thoroughly sieved fruits until they had taken on the consistency of a dense applesauce. Its ascendancy was also aided by an agricultural depression in the 1880s that saw British fruit farmers desperate for new outlets for their produce, and cheap manufactured jam soon flooded the market and became a staple among poorer families.

Marmalade seems to have been a preserve exclusive to Mrs Hudson's and Dr Watson's Scottish forebears until it was introduced into England in the 1870s. There are several legends as to its origin. One of them concerns Mary Queen of Scots and an exhausting journey she made from Scotland to France in 1548. Upon arrival she was comforted with a tasty conserve of oranges specially created for her by a French chef. She enjoyed it so much that it eventually became known as "Marie Malade." Another legend concerns a large cargo of Seville oranges brought into Dundee harbour by a storm-buffeted Spanish vessel in the eighteenth century. An enterprising Scot by the name of James Keller saw a bargain and bought a large quantity cheaply, but was disappointed to find they were too bitter for resale. He turned them over to his wife, who then created the preserve that was to assume a right of place alongside the eggcup and the toast rack at 221b Baker Street and countless other breakfast tables across the nation.

Dr Watson was often to complain of the fumes created by his fellow lodger with his chemical apparatus, and in some of those noxious moments, he may have escaped below to where the air was wholesome and rich with the delectable aromas of Mrs Hudson's cooking. Any efforts put into making one of the sauces or preserves in this chapter will allow a cook—as much as or more than with most culinary exercises—to re-create the authentic scents and flavours of the cuisine enjoyed by Holmes and Watson. An additional reward is the possibility of storing some of them for long periods, and enjoying them again on other occasions. 🦂

Bull Inn Blackcurrant Jam

*It was nearly six o'clock before we found ourselves in the pretty
Surrey village of Esher, with Inspector Baynes as our companion.*

*Holmes and I had taken things for the night, and found comfort-
able quarters at the Bull.*

THE ADVENTURE OF WISTERIA LODGE

The Bull in rural Surrey is just one of the many inns Holmes
and Watson were to stay in during their investigations.
Blackcurrant jam, made from local berries, would have been
one of the condiments with which their hosts graced the breakfast table on such occasions.

Makes 12–15 half-pint (250 mL) jam jars

> 12 cups (3 L) blackcurrants
> 6 cups (1.5 L) water
> 10 cups (2.5 L) superfine sugar
> 2 tbsp (25 mL) unsalted butter

Wash and drain the blackcurrants, making sure that all bits
of stem are removed. Put the blackcurrants and water in a large
saucepan. Cover and simmer gently for 20 minutes or until tender. Stir in the sugar and, when it is dissolved, bring the jam to
a boil.

Boil 20–25 minutes or until the setting point is reached. Test
by dropping a small amount onto a chilled plate. If it forms a
skin and wrinkles to the touch as it cools, then the jam is ready.
Remove from heat and stir in the butter. Skim any scum off the
top of the jam; leave the jam to cool for 15 minutes. Pour it into
warm sterilized jars and seal. Process by the hot-water method
described in the Appendix. ❦

Ginger Brandy Marmalade

"The game's up, Ryder," said Holmes, quietly. "Hold up, man, or you'll be into the fire. Give him an arm back into his chair, Watson. He's not got blood enough to go in for felony with impunity. Give him a dash of brandy. So! Now he looks a little more human. What a shrimp it is, to be sure!"

THE ADVENTURE OF THE BLUE CARBUNCLE

A dash of brandy renewed James Ryder, thief of the Countess of Morcar's precious Blue Carbuncle, long enough to make a full confession to Holmes. The dash of brandy in Ginger Brandy Marmalade may not spark any confessions, but it makes this already tasty conserve quite distinctive.

Makes about 14 cups (3.5 L)

    2 1/2 lb (1.25 kg) Seville oranges (about 6–7
        medium oranges)
    1 lemon
    1 inch (2.5 cm) fresh ginger, peeled and finely chopped
    12 cups (3 L) water
    10 cups (2.5 L) superfine sugar
    1 1/2 cups (375 mL) finely chopped preserved ginger
    2 tbsp (25 mL) brandy

Wash the oranges and lemon and with a sharp knife remove the peel without cutting into the bitter pith. Cut the peel into strips and set aside. Cut the fruit in half. Remove the pith and the pits and place them in a cheesecloth bag along with the ginger. Put the bag into a large pot with the water. Chop the fruit roughly and add it to the pot. Add the strips of peel.

Bring to a boil, cover, and simmer 1 1/2–2 hours, or until the peel is soft enough to disintegrate when squeezed between the finger and the thumb. Remove the cheesecloth bag and stir in the sugar and preserved ginger. Stir until the sugar is dissolved. Bring to a boil and continue boiling, uncovered, 20–25 minutes or until the setting point is reached. Test by dropping a little marmalade on a chilled plate. If a skin forms and the marmalade wrinkles to the touch as it cools, it is ready. Alternatively, boil the marmalade until a floating thermometer registers 220°F (105°C).

Skim any scum from the marmalade. Allow the marmalade to cool for 15 minutes, then gently stir in the brandy. Pour into warm sterilized jars and seal. Process by the hot-water method described in the Appendix.

Note: Pectin acts as the setting agent in jams and marmalades. Most pectin in oranges and lemons is found in the pith and the pits. If the oranges used have very few seeds, then commercial pectin may be required to achieve a proper set. Follow the instructions provided on the package. 🐦

Dr Watson's
Favourite Chutney

"You have been in Afghanistan, I perceive."
"How on earth did you know that?" I asked in astonishment.
"Never mind," said he, chuckling to himself.

A STUDY IN SCARLET

*A*nd so begins the first encounter of Sherlock Holmes with his faithful chronicler, Dr Watson. Watson had indeed been in Afghanistan. He went there from Bombay with the Fifth Northumberland Fusiliers when the second Afghan war broke out. Wounded in the battle of Maiwand, he was removed to the base hospital in Peshawar, and later sent back to England. When he met Holmes he was "thin as a lath and as brown as a nut," and waiting for his health to improve.

Although his days in India and Afghanistan were not always easy, Watson's palate must have been delighted by some of the condiments, such as chutneys, that were native to that part of the Empire's possessions. Below is Dr Watson's own chutney recipe, something he might have experimented with in the idle hours of his convalescence. It is a delicious apple, ginger, and walnut mixture that is good with curries as well as cold meats and cheese.

Makes about 10 half-pint (250 mL) jars

10 medium cooking apples, peeled and chopped
3 medium onions, chopped
1 1/2 cups (375 mL) raisins
2 cups (500 mL) malt vinegar
4 cups (1 L) loosely packed brown sugar
3 tbsp (50 mL) chopped fresh mint
1 1/2 tsp (7 mL) ground coriander
1 tsp (5 mL) cayenne pepper
1 tsp (5 mL) dry mustard
1 tsp (5 mL) salt
1 inch (2.5 cm) fresh ginger, peeled and finely chopped
2 cups (500 mL) chopped walnuts

Put the apples, onions, and raisins in a large stainless steel saucepan. With a wooden spoon, stir in 1 cup (250 mL) of the malt vinegar. Bring to a boil, then simmer, uncovered, until fruit is soft (8–10 minutes). Add the remaining vinegar, sugar, mint, coriander, cayenne, mustard, and salt. Simmer, stirring occasionally, until thick (30–45 minutes), then add the ginger and walnuts. Cook for 2 minutes more.

Pour chutney into warm sterilized jars and seal. Process by the hot-water method described in the Appendix. The taste of your chutney will improve as it ages, and although you may use it shortly after bottling, it will be better if you wait for at least two months before trying it. ❦

Lemon Curd

The landlady had become so accustomed to my late habits that my place had not been laid nor my coffee prepared. With the unreasonable petulance of mankind I rang the bell and gave a curt intimation that I was ready. Then I picked up a magazine from the table and attempted to while away the time with it, while my companion munched silently at his toast.

A STUDY IN SCARLET

$\mathcal{D}$r Watson's mention of Holmes munching silently on his toast occurs early in their association. Watson was to learn a great deal about his fellow lodger's habits, but unfortunately we are left with no detail as to what conserve the Great Detective preferred on his toast. One good probability is lemon curd, a very tasty spread that Mrs Hudson, with her Scottish talent for thrift, could have also used as a tart or Swiss roll filling.

Lemon curd is not a preserve in the strict sense of the word, as it includes ingredients other than fruit and a preservative.

Makes about 1 cup (250 mL)

3/4 cup (175 mL) superfine sugar
1/3 cup (75 mL) unsalted butter
Juice of 2 lemons (4 tbsp/50 mL)
4 egg yolks, well beaten
1 tbsp (15 mL) grated lemon zest

Combine the sugar, butter, lemon juice, and egg yolks in a heatproof bowl or top of a double boiler. Cook over boiling water until the mixture thickens enough to coat the back of a wooden spoon. The curd will thicken further as it cools. Pour into a small bowl and stir in the lemon zest. Store in a covered pot or jar. It will keep for several weeks in the refrigerator. 🍏

Worcestershire Sauce

*"Most singular!" said the distant voice. "Most remarkable! I much
fear, my dear Watson, that there is no return train tonight. I have
unwittingly condemned you to the horrors of a country inn."*

THE ADVENTURE OF THE RETIRED COLOURMAN

The horrors Sherlock Holmes is referring to have to do with
Watson's overnight stay in Little Purlington, a village he
describes as "the most primitive in England." However primitive it was, and whatever Watson suffered by way of accommo-
dation and the food a Little Purlington innkeeper might put
before him, he was assured of a variety of preserves and sauces
that would have mitigated its abominations. One of the most
commonly available was Worcestershire sauce. Sir Baron Sandy
of Worcestershire brought the recipe back with him from India
and later gave it to Mr Lea of Lea and Perrins, who began man-
ufacturing it on a large scale in 1838.

The sauce in this recipe is more piquant than most store-
bought Worcestershire sauces. It is not difficult to make and
could be an interesting gift for friends or relatives.

Makes about 2 cups (500 mL)

1/4 cup (50 mL) chopped shallots
4 cloves garlic, chopped
2 1/2 cups (625 mL) malt vinegar
2 tsp (10 mL) grated fresh horseradish
2 tsp (10 mL) cayenne pepper
1 inch (2.5 cm) fresh ginger, chopped
8 black peppercorns
6 whole cloves
4 cardamom seeds
1/4 cup (50 mL) soy sauce
3 tbsp (50 mL) corn syrup
2 tbsp (25 mL) blackstrap molasses
1 tsp (5 mL) anchovy paste

Put the shallots and garlic in a saucepan with the vinegar, bring to a boil, then simmer, covered, for 20 minutes. Add the horseradish, cayenne, ginger, peppercorns, cloves, cardamom, soy sauce, corn syrup, molasses, and anchovy paste. Stir well and bring to a boil again, then simmer, covered, for 30 minutes. Let the mixture cool, then pour it into a jar with a tight-fitting lid. Leave the mixture for one month, shaking it occasionally.

Strain the sauce through a fine sieve into a bottle with a screw cap or cork. It may be stored in the refrigerator indefinitely.

Worcestershire sauce goes well with an almost unlimited number of foods. ❦

Diogenes Club Béchamel Sauce

We had reached Pall Mall as we talked, and were walking down it from the St James's end. Sherlock Holmes stopped at a door some little distance from the Carlton, and, cautioning me not to speak, he led me into the hall. Through the glass panelling I caught a glimpse of a large and luxurious room in which a considerable number of men were sitting about and reading papers, each in his own little nook.

THE ADVENTURE OF THE GREEK INTERPRETER

Watson is describing the Diogenes Club, of which Holmes's brother, Mycroft, was a member. This recipe for béchamel sauce is based on one devised by Charles Francatelli, who served as Queen Victoria's chef and worked at the Reform Club. It is a Victorian béchamel sauce and as such is more highly flavoured than its contemporary namesake, which is made with a roux and milk. It no doubt made the rounds of all the better clubs in Pall Mall, including the Diogenes.

Makes 2 1/2 cups (625 mL)

2 tbsp (25 mL) butter
1/4 cup (50 mL) all-purpose flour
Pinch nutmeg
1 1/2 cups (375 mL) chicken stock
3/4 cup (150 mL) table (18%) cream
Salt and white pepper

Melt the butter in a saucepan over a low heat. Add the flour, stirring for 2 minutes. Blend in the nutmeg. Slowly add the stock and then the cream, stirring continuously until the sauce thickens. Add the salt and white pepper to taste. Let cool. The sauce can be stored up to 4 days in the refrigerator. It may be used as a sauce base for fish, egg, vegetable, and chicken dishes.

Note: A good chicken stock can be made by simmering, without stirring, a 2–3 lb (1–1.5 kg) stewing chicken for 3 hours in 8–10 cups (2–2.5 L) of water with a sliced carrot, an onion studded with 4 cloves, a bay leaf, a sprig of thyme, three parsley stalks, and 2 tsp (10 mL) of salt. Strain. It will keep up to 4 days, covered, in the refrigerator or up to 3 months if frozen. 🍎

Cumberland Game Sauce

There were a couple of brace of cold woodcock, a pheasant, a pâté-
de-foie-gras *pie, with a group of ancient and cobwebby bottles ...*

THE ADVENTURE OF THE NOBLE BACHELOR

When Holmes felt a game dinner necessary on short notice
for guests he and Watson were entertaining, he had it brought
in from a local confectioner (a dealer in cooked foods and pas-
tries). It would have been unfair to expect Mrs Hudson to
arrange something of this order immediately. Yet she often
cooked game for her lodgers, and the meal was probably com-
plemented by Cumberland game sauce. This recipe comes from
Escoffier's *Le Guide Culinaire*.

Makes about 1 cup (250 mL)

> 1 medium lemon
> 1 medium orange
> 1 tsp (5 mL) hot dry mustard
> Pinch cayenne pepper
> Pinch ginger
> 1/2 cup (125 mL) port

1/4 cup (50 mL) red currant jelly

2 tsp (10 mL) blanched chopped shallots (optional)

Grate the zest of the lemon and the orange. Put the grated zest in a saucepan with enough water to cover and boil for 3 minutes. Drain in a sieve and rinse with cold water. Set aside.

Squeeze the juice from the orange and half of the lemon into the saucepan. You should have about 2 tbsp (25 mL) of juice. Whisk in the mustard, cayenne, and ginger. Add the port and red currant jelly, and stir over medium heat until the jelly dissolves. Squeeze any water out of the blanched shallots (if using) and stir them into the sauce. Simmer, uncovered, for 5 minutes.

Strain the sauce through a sieve into a bowl and stir in the lemon and orange zest. Let cool, then refrigerate until chilled.

Cumberland Sauce is traditionally served with game, as well as ham and lamb. When tightly covered it can be stored indefinitely in the refrigerator. ❦

Cold Partridge Sauce

"There is a cold partridge on the sideboard, Watson, and a bottle of Montrachet. Let us renew our energies before we make a fresh call upon them."

THE ADVENTURE OF THE VEILED LODGER

This is an adaptation of a nineteenth-century recipe and is likely very similar to the one Mrs Hudson would have served with cold fowl.

Makes about 1/2 cup (125 mL)

> 4 hard-boiled egg yolks
> 1 anchovy (or 1/2 tsp/2 mL anchovy paste)
> 2 green onions, white part only
> 1 1/2 tsp (7 mL) sugar
> 1 tsp (5 mL) dry mustard
> Pinch cayenne pepper
> 2 tbsp (25 mL) white wine vinegar
> 1/3 cup (75 mL) olive oil

The traditional method used to create this sauce is to pound the egg yolks, anchovy, onion, sugar, mustard, and cayenne in a mortar, then gradually work in the vinegar followed by the oil. A contemporary alternative is to put all the ingredients in a blender and blend until smooth.

This sauce can be served with any cold poultry or game bird. It will keep in the refrigerator up to 4 days. ❦

Appendix:
Preserving Method

The jam, marmalade, and chutney preserves in this book must all undergo heat sterilization to prevent bacterial contamination. Follow this simple procedure.

1. Use canning jars and lids that are sold in supermarkets and hardware stores rather than recycled food jars. They offer a better seal.

2. Wash the jars and lids with dish soap and hot water. Rinse them, then sterilize them in boiling water that completely covers them for 10 minutes. Remove the jars with tongs and stand on a clean tea towel. If preserving immediately, leave the lids in the water until needed. Otherwise dry them on the clean tea towel as well.

3. Leave 1/4 inch (5 mm) of head space in the jars after pouring in the hot preserve.

4. Wipe the jar rim with a clean cloth, then secure the snap lid on the jar and apply the metal screw band.

5. Place the jars on a rack in a canner or large stockpot. Add hot water to cover the jars by 2 inches (5 cm).

6. Cover the pot and bring the water to a boil. Continue to boil for 20 minutes.

7. Remove the jars and leave them to cool for 12 hours.

8. Remove the screw bands and store the preserves in a cool, dry place.

Note: As the jars cool they may make a popping sound. This is an indication that the jar is firmly sealed and is nothing to worry about. ❦

Bibliography

Ayrton, Elisabeth. *English Provincial Cooking*, Mitchell Beazley, 1980

Bailey, Adrian. *The Cooking of the British Isles*, Time-Life Books, 1969

Beeton, Isabella. *Book of Household Management*, 1861; Chancellor Press, 1982

Berriedale-Johnson, Michelle. *The Victorian Cookbook*, Sheldrake, 1989

Brown, Catherine. *Scottish Cookery*, Richard Drew, 1985

Burton, R. Bessie, and Ella J. Wells. *Compendium of Cookery and Reliable Recipes*, Jewell & Co., 1890

Davies, Jennifer. *The Victorian Kitchen*, BBC Books, 1991

De la Falaise, Maxime. *Seven Centuries of English Cooking*, McGraw-Hill, 1973; Grove Press, 1992

Doyle, Sir Arthur Conan. *Complete Sherlock Holmes and Other Detective Stories*, HarperCollins, 1994

Drummond, J.C., and Anne Wilbraham. *The Englishman's Food*, Jonathan Cape, 1939; Pimlico, 1994

Escoffier, A. *Le Guide Culinaire*, 1903; Flammarion, 1921

Francatelli, Charles. *The Modern Cook*, 1846; Dover and Constable, 1973

Harrison, Michael. *The London of Sherlock Holmes*, David & Charles Newton Abbot, 1972

Isitt, Verity. *Take a Buttock of Beefe*, Headline, 1989

Kitchiner, Dr W. *The Cook's Oracle*, Robert Cadell, Edinburgh, 1840

Mabey, David and Rose. *Jams, Pickles and Chutneys*, Macmillan London, 1975

Mennell, Stephen. *All Manners of Food*, Basil Blackwell, 1985

Miall, Antony and Peter. *The Victorian Christmas Book*, Dent, 1978

Miles, Clement A. *Christmas Customs and Traditions*, T. Fisher Unwin, 1912; Dover 1976

Thomson, John. *Victorian London Street Life*, S. Low, Marston, Searle & Rivington, 1877; Dover 1994

Thomson, June. *Holmes and Watson*, Constable, 1995

Viney, Charles. *Sherlock Holmes in London*, Colour Library Books, 1995

Warren, Janet. *A Feast of Scotland*, Hodder & Stoughton, 1979; Treasure Press, 1986

Wilson, C. Anne. *Food and Drink in Britain*, Constable, 1973

Recipe Index

General Index

Hogarth, William, 159
Holmes, Mycroft, 56, 81, 128, 182
Holmes, Sherlock;
    acting training, 93-4; class back-
    ground, 42, 46, 61; disguises, ix, 12,
    31, 38, 91-2, 94, 95; favourite
    restaurants, 62, 92; fluency in
    French, 96; French ancestry, 12,
    148; health, 64, 162; meets Queen
    Victoria, 169; on Mrs Hudson's
    cooking viii; university days, 52, 56,
    122, 139; Yorkshire roots, 42, 72,
    137
Horner, Jack, 152
Hound of the Baskervilles, The 3, 32, 76,
    130
Hudson, Mrs
    and fishmongers, 39; and green-
    grocers, 19; patience, 161; Scottish
    cuisine, viii
Illustrious Client, The 66
Industrial Revolution, 72
Inspector Lestrade, 68
James V of Scotland, 12
Jones, Inigo, 17
Le Guide Culinaire 184
Man with the Twisted Lip, The 17, 88, 92
Mary of Guise-Lorraine, 12
Mary Queen of Scots, 138, 171
Mazarin Stone, The 70
Meat, 61-3;
    Anglo-Saxon, 62; livestock improve-
    ments, 63; medieval, 63; Norman
    influence, 62; offal (internal
    organs), 62; preferences for beef,
    61-2; refrigeration and canning, 63,
    70; transportation, 63; Smithfield
    market, 63
Modern Cook, The 169
Musgrave Ritual, The 24, 56, 122
Naval Treaty, The viii, 54, 84
Noble Bachelor, The vii, 39, 157, 184
Poultry and Game, 43-5;
    aristocracy and venison, 45; August
    grouse shoot, 45, 46; birds of
    choice, 44-5; Company of Poulters,

44; enclosed game parks, 45; fal-
conry, 44; fowlers, 44; Roman influ-
ences, 44; transportation to mar-
kets, 43
Prince Albert of Saxe-Coborg 22, 137
Priory School, The 72, 100
Queen Victoria ix, 10, 22, 80, 81, 82,
    137, 169, 182
Red-Headed League, The 22, 105
Reform Club ix, 169, 182
Reichenbach Fall 12, 91
Reigate Squire, The 162
Resident Patient, The 36
Retired Colourman, The 80, 180
Salads and Vegetables, 17-19;
    class attitudes towards, 18, 19;
    estate gardens, 19; green-grocers,
    19, 20; imported vegetables, 18, 19;
    kitchen gardens, 19, 26; market
    gardens, 17, 18; mushroom cultiva-
    tion 24; Roman influences on, 18
Sandwich, Earl of, 105
Sauces and Preserves, 169-72;
    at Buckingham Palace, 169-70;
    bottled sauces, 170; fruit solids, 170
    jam, 171; marmalade, history of,
    171-2; oriental influences, 170
Scandal in Bohemia, A 6, 78, 94, 95, 132
Shaw, George Bernard, xi
Shoscombe Old Place 32, 38
Sign of Four, The 5, 10, 29, 50, 92, 164
Silver Blaze 102
Simpson's-in-the-Strand viii, 61, 66,
    92
Six Napoleons, The 152, 161
Soups, 3-5;
    Anglo-Saxon, 4; dried, 5; French
    influences, 4; gruels and pottages,
    4; in Holme's day, 4; Lord Mayor's
    turtle soup, 4; "portable", 5
Soyer, Alexis viii, ix
Speckled Band, The 86
Spitalfields market, 17, 19
Stockbroker's Clerk, The 79, 104
Study in Scarlet, A 68, 74, 144,
    165, 176, 178

195